OUT OF SIGHT

JOE BOLLARD was born in the 1930s in Dublin's inner city. One of thirteen children, he became blind at the age of two. Four years later, his family moved to Liverpool and Joe was sent to St Vincent's School for the Blind in West Derby, where he became a star pupil. Having trained as a mat-maker against his wishes, Joe decided to devote himself to his real love — music. In 1957 he returned to Ireland as pianist with the Ballina-based Jack Ruane Band, with whom he toured throughout Ireland and in England and the US. He left in 1964 to devote more time to his wife and children, and worked for many years as resident keyboard player at The Silver Tassie in Loughlinstown, Co. Dublin, and at the Dalkey Island Hotel. For some years he was a DJ on pirate radio, and he went on to work with RTÉ's *Listen and See*, and latterly *Audioscope*. He has been involved in several fund-raising cycles in aid of the National Council for the Blind of Ireland, whose audio magazine he edits. The cycles on the back of a tandem have taken him to the US, Europe, Australia, Africa and Canada. He and his wife live in Bray where he has been organist at his local parish church for over thirty years.

Out of Sight

Joe Bollard

WOLFHOUND PRESS

First published in 1997 by
Wolfhound Press Ltd
68 Mountjoy Square
Dublin 1, Ireland
Tel: (353-1) 874 0354
Fax: (353-1) 872 0207

British Library Cataloguing in Publication Data
A catalogue record for this book is available from the British Library.

ISBN 0-86327-623-7

10 9 8 7 6 5 4 3 2 1

Photographs in photo section courtesy of the Bollard family
Cover Photograph and final picture in photo section: Mike O'Toole
Cover Design: Slick Fish Design
Typesetting: Wolfhound Press
Printed in the Republic of Ireland by Colour Books, Dublin.

To Marjorie Quarton,
without whose help and support
this book would not have been written.

And to my sister, Margaret,
who never got the thanks
she deserved from us all.

Out of Sight

And would he like another cup of tea?
Or would he like another piece of bread?
It's strange — they always seem to ask my friends,
They never seem to want to talk to me.

The social worker keeps me on her file,
If I question her she thinks I'm being defiant,
She greets me with a patronising smile,
To her I'm not a person — I'm a client.

There are some who think that I'm not just quite right,
Mentally retarded being blind,
Perhaps they think because I'm out of sight,
They figure that I'm also out of mind.

Joe Bollard
September 1997

~ One ~

I was crying. I wanted to pee, I didn't like my scratchy new jumper and trousers — they made me itch. I was four years old and I didn't want to go to school.

My mother held onto my left hand, while in my right I clutched a bag of biscuits. I dragged my feet as we made our way up the drive of St Mary's School for the Blind in Merrion, Dublin.

I should have been excited, for today I'd had my first ride on a tram. We'd left Pearse House flats and taken a number 8 tram to Merrion. I'd put on my new clothes — they smelled of mothballs, yuck — and I had new shoes that squeaked when I walked, but they hurt my toes. I had my very own handkerchief and my mother had warned me not to wipe my nose on my sleeve. 'It's not nice,' she said.

I should have been excited. But I wasn't — I was thoroughly miserable. I wanted to go back to the flats, to the familiar sounds of horses and cars, the City Quay Church bell ringing out and my pals playing football and fighting. But what I missed most was the familiar smell, the smell of the flats, a smell that I later learned to recognise as the smell of poverty.

I've had an acute sense of smell as long as I can remember, and as we went through the big front door I noticed a different smell — of floor polish and cabbage. There's a widely held theory, one which I don't altogether agree with, that losing one of your senses automatically improves the other four. I have a very keen sense of hearing, but I don't know whether I hear better than some of my seeing friends. I do know that my sense of smell is unusually keen. Even when I dream, I can often pick up the scent of my surroundings.

Entering the school hallway, I felt — or I should say, I smelt — a presence beside me, and then I heard her voice. 'Is this our new young man?' she asked.

'Yes, Sister, this is Joseph Bollard,' my mother answered. Now I was really puzzled. This sister person, smelling of disinfectant and peppermints, couldn't possibly be my sister. Maggie, Sue and Vera, my three sisters, were at home, and I wanted to go home too.... Oh, wait a minute, she must be my mother's sister.

'Don't cry now, be a brave little soldier and we'll take you into the next room and meet some more new people,' Sister Peppermints said.

'I want to do me pooley!' I bawled, wiping my nose on my sleeve. My mother released my hand and Sister Peppermints (I later discovered she was called Sister Acquin) led me into a room from the corner of which came a whirring noise.

'Now, ladies, here is our new little man,' she said.

The whirring stopped and a woman came rushing towards me and grabbed me in a bear hug.

'Oh, isn't he very thin!' she cried. 'Never mind, we'll soon change that.'

Then Sister Peppermints whispered something to her and moved silently away.

'Come and see what we have here.' The woman steered me in the direction of the corner where I had heard the whirring sound. 'Do you know what this is?' she enquired, placing my hand on a wheel connected to a belt. 'It's a sewing machine,' she said, answering her own question.

Running my hand along the belt, I found it was connected to a pedal. I began to press the pedal and, following the belt with my hand, I felt the wheel flying round. I put my hand farther around and immediately felt a sharp jab from a needle. It pierced deep into my thumb and I shrieked with pain. I could feel blood gushing out as the woman tried to grab my hand, but I wouldn't let her. Sister Peppermints came running in and began to scold the woman for allowing a blind child to play with a sewing machine.

Meanwhile, I wiped my eyes and my nose on my sleeve and the woman chastised me for spreading blood all over my face.

'I want me mammy!' I screamed, jumping up and down on the spot.

'Now, now, be a brave little soldier,' Sister Peppermints said. 'You'll see your mammy again very soon.' Suddenly it dawned on me that she meant that Mammy was gone: gone home to the flats, gone and left me with these strangers. I took a deep breath, screamed at the top of my voice, danced, kicked and then deliberately wet my trousers.

I must have looked a mess with tears running down my blood-streaked face, pooley running down my legs into my new shoes, blood on my new *geansaí*, mouth open, arms flailing, and screaming *double forte*.

Sister Peppermints took it all in her stride. She picked me up, tucked me under her arm, and carried me, kicking and squealing, into the school.

* * *

That first night, I lay in bed, miserable, thinking about my family and wondering whether they were thinking about me. At last, I cried myself to sleep. Of course, I realise now that there must have been other children homesick and crying, but I was too young and too wrapped up in my own misery to care.

When I woke up in the morning I had no idea where I was, and I heard this dreadful squealing — I was terrified, I had never heard a noise like it before. One of the girls came to my cot (I slept in a bed at home but here we all had cots). She had been designated to look after me and I soon discovered that she was blind too. She was supposed to dress me, but was surprised to find that I could dress myself. She brought me to the lavatory and showed me where the lavatory, handbasin and towel rail were. I dressed and washed in silence, refusing to speak. I was still heartbroken.

I learned later that the squealing came from the pigs on the farm owned by the school. It was a regular sound, which woke us up every day. Being blind and coming from the inner city, I had no idea what a pig looked or sounded like. Most kids of my age would at least have seen a picture of a pig. I hadn't a clue.

* * *

My first days at St Mary's were spent crying, throwing tantrums and wetting my trousers. I was as obnoxious as possible, hoping, I suppose, that they would send me home.

In those days, hugging and kissing small children wasn't usual outside the immediate family, and I missed the warmth and cuddles I was used to getting from my brothers and sisters. A girl had been told to dress me on my first morning, but there was no question of her playing the big sister. Isolated by blindness, I was, I felt, quite alone.

Eventually however, I must have come to my senses. Always happiest in a crowd, I settled down and made friends. I can't remember how or when, but suddenly it seemed that I was a favourite with everyone in the school.

I also started to learn very quickly. I don't remember learning Braille, but apparently I picked it up fast. One thing I do remember was finding it strange that most people there were blind. Also strange was the amount of space everywhere. Then there were the smells. Always there was the floor polish, and smells of cooking, particularly cabbage, disinfectant, and some of the older ladies smelt rather peculiar I thought.

* * *

As well as being a school for blind girls and boys, St Mary's had a section for elderly blind ladies. Many of the girls and ladies played in the orchestra, and every so often they gave a concert. This was sheer joy for me and I remember listening in wonder to the lovely musical sounds.

Music has always been an integral part of my life — I couldn't function without it. I use music all the time and it serves many purposes for me: turning me on, turning me off, stirring me, relaxing me, soothing, arousing, making me laugh or weep. For me, music is a tonic and better than any tranquilliser. My musical tastes are very wide — classical, big band, jazz, folk — and my record and CD collection is huge.

I didn't start actually to play until I was twelve, by which time I had left St Mary's. However, I have always been a singer. I sing all the time. I hum to myself when I'm on my own, and I sing around the house. This can be annoying for other people, especially when someone is laying down the law to me and I keep singing! Often I don't even know I'm doing it.

Even in those early days at St Mary's, I would wander around the school singing. I'm told that there was one snatch of a song I would sing: 'Rum-tiddly-um-tum-tum, here comes the man with the mandolin' — only with my strong Dublin accent it was the 'man with a mandoleeun'.

* * *

At St Mary's I soon learned my way around. I'd learned mobility at home and I had no fear of crashing into things but was a typical, healthy kid. I scrambled, jumped, ran, fell, slipped, bumped and scraped my knees, banged my forehead, bled my nose, cut my fingers — all the things that any youngster of four or five will do.

I was also extremely curious about everything — as indeed I still am. I have to know what makes things tick, what things feel like. Once this was literally my downfall. There was a big playground at St Mary's, at the end of which was a large statue of the Virgin Mary holding the Child Jesus in her arms. This statue was huge to me, stretching up into the sky. I was anxious to know what the top of the statue was like and to feel the Baby Jesus. One afternoon I climbed up the statue, digging my toes into the stand, stretching up, gripping the blessed Virgin's legs with my knees, reaching up further and grabbing her around the waist, and finally pulling myself right up onto her shoulders, so that I could feel the Baby Jesus.

One of the nuns must have spotted me from the window. I was actually sitting on top of the blessed Virgin's head with my legs hanging down when I got this almighty whack across the backside. I let go and fell, crashing down onto the concrete, splitting my nose, and squealing just like one of the pigs.

Not one of my happier experiences, but it didn't cure me of my curiosity and determination to find out about everything.

~ Two ~

I became blind before I was two years old. I don't care for the expression to 'lose one's sight' — anyway, I didn't lose mine, it was taken from me.

I believe I was a bright, talkative toddler, number ten in a family of thirteen. My father worked as a builder's labourer and we lived in a big house in the inner city, which we shared with other families, my mother acting as caretaker for the house. At the time I'm writing about, she was pregnant with her eleventh child.

I can remember waking one night and screaming and screaming. My mother thought I was just teething and tried to soothe me. She relied on aspirin and elastoplast as a cure for most ills. If you became obviously seriously ill, you would be rushed down to the clinic. I suppose that was what happened to me. When all efforts to quieten my screams failed, I was wrapped in a blanket and my parents ran with me to Sir Patrick Dun's, our nearest hospital.

Probably I will never know the exact truth of what happened next. Apparently I was diagnosed as having meningitis and was kept in for tests. My parents were told to go away for three days and then come back for the results. It's hard to believe that they agreed to this, but both of them had a deeply ingrained respect for professionals, such as doctors, whom they obeyed without question.

Now comes the mystery. I was told when I was older that I had a mastoid, not meningitis, and that when operating on it, the surgeon accidentally severed the optic nerve. I have been assured many times that this is anatomically impossible. It seems more likely that the 'accident' was a misdiagnosis and that I was for several days being treated as a meningitis patient, resulting in the mastoid being neglected, so that an abscess may have formed at the base of my brain. In pre-penicillin days, such an abscess could have been very dangerous and could easily have resulted in the loss of my sight.

In any case, my mother returned three days later and was shocked to see no reaction when she approached my cot. I just lay still.

'What's wrong with Joe?' she asked the nurse on the ward.

'I can't say, but I'll get a doctor and you can speak to him.'

My mother tells me that I cried and asked her to turn on the light. It was the middle of the day so she knew something was badly wrong and was half-prepared.

When the doctor arrived, he was very apologetic. 'I'm sorry, Mrs Bollard, there has been a dreadful mishap. Your little boy is blind.'

My mother who, as I have said, was pregnant with my baby sister at the time, went into shock. She rushed home to tell the news to the rest of the family. My grandmother was living with us then, and when she saw my mother's face, she knew that something was seriously amiss. She asked what was wrong but my mother had lost her speech with the shock. Granny thought she must be going into premature labour, and my brother was dispatched immediately to fetch my father from work. He arrived to find Mother in the bedroom with Granny holding her, trying to find out what was causing her such distress. She was trying to say, 'Joe is blind', but no sound came out. In the end she wrote it down and the whole family burst into tears. All except my father, who grabbed his coat and ran at full speed to the hospital.

I am one of those lucky people who have been blessed with a very good memory. I can remember being able to see. When I am really over-tired, just before I fall asleep, pictures rush before my subconscious. I can remember colours — red, blue, green — although pink or purple would mean nothing to me. I can't remember faces though, which perhaps is why they mean little to me today.

Screaming with pain and trying to bang my head on the wall is my first clear memory. The next is lying in my cot in the hospital and hearing my father shouting and bellowing at what I presume was a doctor. Now, my father in full flight bellowing and shouting had to be heard to be believed — it was dreadful. I believe it would have measured 8.5 on the Richter scale! He never had to slap us — he just roared and we jumped and obeyed immediately, whatever the command.

What happened next is vague. I was in hospital for some time, feeling terribly afraid and wanting to go home. I have a half memory of being lifted out of my cot and wheeled home in a pram.

* * *

My resentment in later life was directed at my parents rather than at the hospital. Whatever negligence or misdiagnosis led to my being blind for the rest of my life wasn't done on purpose — it was just an accident with devastating results. I don't bear any grudge or ill will towards the people concerned. But certainly there must have been negligence, as the surgeon who operated on my mastoid paid for my early education at St Mary's. If he had been personally responsible, I doubt whether he would have admitted liability by doing this, but he must have felt that some compensation was in order.

When I asked my mother why she and my father did nothing, she said, 'We didn't want to.' Knowing them, I can understand their attitude, but I certainly don't go along with it.

My mother was not an educated woman. Born in Cork, she left school at the age of twelve to work in the cotton mills where, for several years, she worked long hours. She could just about read and write. She met my father, who was in the army, when she was twenty, and soon married him and started her large family. She and my father firmly believed in the 'Us and Them' system — we being the poor, the working class, the second-class citizens. 'They' were the doctors, priests, teachers, policemen — anyone in authority. You never challenged these people or questioned their decisions. After my father's noisy outburst in the hospital, he must have decided to make the best of it.

I have often felt that had my parents taken an action against the hospital, the resulting compensation could have set me up for life — things might have been easier for me later on if I'd had financial stability; but they didn't and I wasn't and they weren't, so I just got on with it.

* * *

I can't remember learning to be blind. When I came home from hospital, my mother said that she hadn't the time 'to sit under a blind child', so I was turfed out to play with the other kids. Probably it was good for me up to a point as I ran around the flats, tumbled over, crashed into things and constantly fell down, cutting and bruising myself. I soon learned the whereabouts of the poles that held up the washing line, the number of balcony steps, the position of the gates — all learned through bumps, bangs and scrapes. I learned to fight my own battles, as the kids in the flats gave me no special treatment. I learned to use my ears and my wits.

I remember playing football too, being able to sense when the ball was coming in my direction, kicking out and sometimes hitting it, sometimes not, shouting and yelling like all the other kids.

The high spot of the summer used to be when my father, an avid fisherman, took us all off to Greystones on the train to camp. Off we would go, the whole family, with tents and fishing rods, food, camping stoves, the lot. We must have looked like the Children of Israel wandering in the desert. We would spend long periods camped on the beach. Those halcyon days at Greystones were a great joy to me, a skinny little boy from the cramped inner-city flats. I was free to clamber over rocks on the beach, to roll around in the sand, to splash about in the sea; getting clean air into my lungs, breathing the smells of the seaside, falling asleep each night to the rhythmic roll of the waves and the rumble of the trains on the tracks not far above the beach where we were camped.

Then back to the flats, where one of my earliest memories is of falling down the stairs. I was playing with a bicycle wheel on the landing, misjudged the distance to the top stair and hurtled, beam over apex, to the bottom. I have still got a scar on my upper lip as a legacy of my first and only attempt at unicycling.

My mother of course treated the cut with disinfectant and sticking plaster, her sovereign remedies. It should have been stitched, which would probably have saved me from being scarred. Still, I can now appreciate her attitude in not wrapping me in cotton wool or guarding me twenty-four hours a day. I ran free, made my own way, stood on my own two feet and, as a result of this therapy, I developed the keen sense of mobility that has remained with me ever since.

* * *

This training stood me in good stead when I went to St Mary's, as I have told, and I became relaxed and confident, and stopped thinking about my home all the time. I stayed there until I was six years old, and then something happened that changed my whole life.

I would go home at holiday time: summer, Christmas and Easter. During one of these holidays I was surprised to hear that my mother was going to join my father in England. He was with the British Army in Liverpool, although he was too old for active service. He had served in the army during and after the First World War.

It was decided that in my mother's absence, her mother should come up from Cork to look after us. I remember the day she arrived: she patted me on the head and gave me a halfpenny for sweets. She smelled strongly of whiskey.

I returned to St Mary's after that holiday and when I next came home, for the summer holidays, I found a remarkable change in our flat. There was very little furniture and we had to sleep on the floor on mattresses. Granny had been selling the furniture to buy drink.

That night, as we lay on our mattresses, my brother Georgie, who was older than I, remarked that he was hungry. So was I, but Georgie told me that Granny locked the press where the bread was kept each night, and that she kept the key around her neck. I told him I thought I could steal the key, so I decided to have a try — I wouldn't have to turn on any lights.

I crept along the floor to where Granny was snoring in a drunken stupor, I reached out, found the key tied around her neck, and managed to get it off. We opened the press and had a good feed, remembering to leave some bread for the morning. I then crept back to Granny's mattress and replaced the key. When she woke up the next morning, she was perplexed to find how little bread was left, but we managed to convince her that she'd given us some before we went to bed. She couldn't blame us for stealing it as she still had the key. She never found out how we got the bread.

Not long after the bread episode, my sister Margaret and my brother Georgie placed me on a sofa which had castors on it and, on Granny's instructions, pushed it through the flats over to Mrs Byrne's. Granny had sold the sofa to Mrs Byrne. I can still recall the thrill of hurtling through Pearse House flats on our sofa, breaking my sides laughing, not realising that our home was slowly being taken apart by our alcoholic granny.

And then it happened, the event that changed our lives. One night there was a knock on the door. The flat was almost bare of furniture and we were all still sitting on the floor, so it must have looked pretty awful to any visitor. When the door opened, there was a shout of delight — it was my mother and father who had come to surprise us.

My mother was totally shocked by the sight that greeted her eyes — she had had no idea that things were so bad. She had been sending money home every week, but Granny had obviously been spending it on drink.

With both of my parents at home seeing the devastation, there was a dreadful row, and within a few days, we all packed bag and baggage and headed for Liverpool. It all happened so quickly. One day we were all sitting on the floor in Dublin, then, in no time at all, we were on the boat to England. I really don't think we could take it all in.

On the day we left, my mother and father just walked out of the flat, with all of us walking behind. We closed the door, leaving Granny lying drunkenly on the mattress in the middle of the kitchen.

* * *

I distinctly remember the journey over to Liverpool. We couldn't sail direct from North Wall, as this longer route to

England was considered too dangerous in wartime, and the only passenger boat was the 'Mail' to Holyhead. We got the train from Westland Row (now Pearse) Station, and sang as we travelled to Dún Laoghaire. The boat trip to Holyhead was quite smooth and we ran wild around the boat, probably upsetting the other passengers. Then we took the train to Chester and changed for Liverpool. When we arrived at Lime Street Station, shattered from travelling, Mother gathered us all together and walked us to our new home at 77A Queen's Road, Everton. I clearly recall that walk. It's a long one at the best of times, but to a six-year-old, wrecked from travelling, it was really dreadful.

We discovered that our new house was really an old house and very shabby. There was a bombed building beside it where the Germans had recently carried out an air raid.

My sister Margaret, who had acted as a mother to us while our parents were in England, went into the house and was immediately bitten by the pet dog, Barney. My two elder brothers, Richard and Michael, had been living in Liverpool with my parents for some time before we arrived, and it was their dog. There were tears all round as we entered the house. As usual, I wanted to go home, I hated this place.

Everywhere there seemed to be a smell of smoke and soot burning. This was 1941 and Liverpool had just come to the end of a very bad blitz. The city had been pounded by German bombers for weeks.

Homesick and weary, I was quickly asleep that night, but was soon awakened by my brother who lifted me out of bed and carried me downstairs. 'Where are you taking me?' I sleepily asked.

'Down to the cellar,' he said.

Suddenly there was a crashing sound from outside.

'The thunder sounds different here from what it does in Ireland,' I remarked.

'That's not thunder,' he told me, 'That's bombs.'

'What's bombs?'

'Germans drop them on you to kill you,' he replied.

I began to yell when I heard this and was still howling when we reached the cellar under our house, which acted as an air-raid shelter. It was a crazy idea, to have a shelter right under the house: if a bomb had fallen on it, we would all have been buried alive. However, we were lucky and, like everything else, we got used to the air raids. I have always thought it strange that, at that time when most people were leaving Liverpool and being evacuated into country areas for safety, the Bollards were moving in!

At the beginning, we all wanted to go back to Dublin — all the children that is. But, strange to relate, some of my brothers and sisters have never been back to Dublin since that day in 1941.

~ Three ~

The first few months in Liverpool were really miserable for all the family. For one thing, our house was infested with fleas. Within a few hours of our arrival, we were all scratching. I think there were lice as well — there were certainly plenty of mice. Apart from this, I have to say that my parents were partly to blame for our poor and wretched state.

We arrived in Liverpool, as I have said, in the middle of the war, when people were trying to carry on with their lives as normally as possible while being constantly hammered by the German blitz. Everyone was under tremendous strain and pressure.

My father was serving in the Engineers, working mainly on cleaning up after the raids and repairing damage. My mother worked in the munitions factory in Kirkby, which is quite a distance from where we lived in Everton. This necessitated a long journey by tram every day. She worked long hours and I'm sure must have earned good money. Unfortunately, my parents spent most of their free time in the pub, as they both drank heavily. As a result, we suffered.

My eldest sister, Margaret, who was no more than thirteen or fourteen when we arrived in Liverpool, had to become a mother to us all. When we lived in Dublin, she was attending school like any other thirteen-year-old, but when we arrived in England she was kept at home to look after the house and the family while my mother went to work. She would get the other children off to school in the morning, clean the house, do the washing, prepare the meals and look after my baby brother, Willie.

These were hard times for all of us children, but we could

at least get out and play, albeit in dirty streets and bombed out houses — bombed 'ollers as they were called. Margaret couldn't get out at all. All her time was spent in the house, looking after the family.

I can well remember our first Christmas in Liverpool. We had no money to buy toys, although my parents must have had money for drink — I remember my mother being quite drunk on Christmas Day. Margaret made a rag doll for my younger sister, Vera; my older brother, Michael, made a horse and cart for baby Willie; the rest of us got nothing.

We wouldn't go out on Christmas Day because we were afraid the other kids would ask us what presents we'd got and we would have been embarrassed to tell them the truth.

On Christmas Eve, my parents went out to the pub, leaving a huge pot on the fire, containing a Christmas pudding that my mother had made. Margaret was given strict instructions to keep an eye on it. We used to make our own entertainment in those days. We had no radio — that came later — so we sat around and sang songs, each one having his or her party piece. The boys in our family were all quite good singers. Michael would do an impression of an Italian tenor. He told us he was singing in Italian but I think he just sang gibberish which sounded like Italian and we believed him. Georgie could do a very good impression of Al Jolson and was a good spoons player. I sat on the coal scuttle, using it as a drum, banging it with two spoons.

That night we were all singing away and completely forgot about the pudding until I said, 'What's that smell?' Then there was panic — the water had boiled off the pudding and it was burned to a cinder. Naturally there was trouble when my parents finally got home, and there was no Christmas pudding that year.

* * *

Following our arrival in Liverpool, I was out of school for about ten months. My brothers and sisters attended St Francis Xavier's School, while I stayed at home and my parents enquired about a school for me. Eventually, after endless sessions at the education offices in Liverpool, it was decided that I would be sent to St Vincent's School for the Blind in West Derby. When I first heard this, I thought I would be coming home each night like the others, but I was soon disillusioned. This was a boarding school, and I would be coming home only three times a year — at Christmas, Easter and in the summer.

For a week or so before I left for school, my mother brought me around the shops buying new clothes for me. She must have taken time off work to do this. Of course, clothes rationing was in force and she must have used up a lot of coupons getting the clothes, which would have cost quite a bit. Everything I got was brand new, including a new suitcase.

Although she had had thirteen children, not including two stillbirths and a number of miscarriages, my mother was an unemotional woman. If she showed any emotion at all, it was anger, and usually in rows with my father. She did, however, cry when my brother Richard was killed in the Middle East in 1948 while serving with the British Army.

When we were children, my mother never told any of us that she loved us, she never hugged or kissed us. The emotional side of my character — and I am a very emotional person — must have come from my father or my grandparents, certainly not from my mother.

The day I left home for St Vincent's, I was terrified. I had just become adjusted to my new home, and stopped missing the Dublin flats. My mother bathed me and dressed me in my new clothes. We had no hot water in the house, so having a bath meant filling the tin bath from big pots heated on the fire, and then sitting in the bath in front of the fire.

On that particular day, everybody else was out of the house — my brothers and sisters would have been at school, my father at work. I don't know where Margaret was. My mother had taken the day off work, and only she and I were there. We were waiting for the 'Education Man' to come, she informed me. I had no idea what she was talking about.

At last, there was a knock on the door and my mother answered it. A man with a posh accent came in and patted me on the head.

'Hello, Joseph,' he said. (This immediately put me off him

— I hate being called Joseph.) 'So we're going to school are we? Well, let's get off then.' He picked up my new suitcase, my mother handed me my gas mask in its square box with a long piece of string which I put around my shoulder, the strange man took my hand, and then — horror of horrors! — I realised that Mother wasn't coming with me.

At that moment, I think I longed for some show of affection as never before. There was nothing doing though. She just ruffled my hair with her hand and said, 'Now, you be a good boy, Joe, won't you?' Wasn't there to be a goodbye kiss, a hug, perhaps? Wouldn't she walk to the end of the road with us? Why wasn't she bringing me to school? I think it would have been a big help to me in coming to terms with leaving home. But she didn't, and I've never forgotten that day.

The Education Man and I walked down Queen's Road onto West Derby Road, we took a 29A tram to the Old Swan, then we changed onto a bus. While we were travelling, the man didn't speak to me at all. I just sat and wondered why my mother hadn't come with me. I made excuses for her. Perhaps she had to get the dinner for the others, I told myself; perhaps she had to do the washing; perhaps she was tired. I was only seven and very lonely. We walked down Yew Tree Lane, turned into a gravelled drive, the man rang the bell by the side of the big front door, and I, Joe Bollard, entered St Vincent's School for the Blind, where I was to remain and which was to influence my life for the next nine years.

* * *

We were admitted through the front door and, as at St Mary's, there was that smell of floor polish. No other smell this time, just floor polish. A nun shuffled towards us. Nuns never walked — they either shuffled or glided. I got the impression sometimes that they were on rubber wheels.

The Education Man spoke in a toneless voice. 'This is the Bollard child,' he said, putting my suitcase down. Then he said something quietly to the nun, and disappeared.

'What's your name, child?' the nun asked.

'Joseph Bollard, Sister,' I replied. I knew she was a nun, even though I couldn't see her — her rosary beads, which hung down by her side, rattled loudly as she moved.

'Come along, Joseph, and we'll introduce you to your new friends. I believe you are from Ireland?'

'Yes, Sister.'

'What school did you go to in Ireland?'

'St Mary's in Merrion.'

'Oh, that's wonderful. I've visited that school many times — most of the nuns here are Irish. Have you any Irish?'

'A little bit, Sister.'

'And I'm sure you know your prayers too. You are a clever little boy. Come along now, don't you cry, you'll see your family again very soon.'

The tears had started. I wanted to go to that home which was only a tram and a bus ride away. Why did I have to stay here? I knew I had to go to school, but why couldn't I go home, even if only at weekends? The floodgates opened and I began to cry.

The school was big and airy, with long, tiled corridors and high ceilings. On my first evening, I hardly spoke to anyone. I was devastated. At tea in the dining room I sat beside a boy who kept asking me questions and passing what little information I gave him on to the rest of the lads at the table. Then we went to the chapel to say the rosary. My thoughts again wandered home and I knew that they would all be sitting around the table having their tea, and I wondered if they were thinking about me. Through the monotonous droning of the whole school saying the rosary, I thought I could hear Margaret's voice. 'Come on Joe, eat your bread, then you can go out and play on the 'ollers with the others.'

After the rosary, we small boys went to bed. I was taken to St Mary's Dormitory. My bed was in a corridor. I undressed and climbed into the narrow bed. It was only half past seven and this was strange for me — at home I was hardly ever in bed before ten o'clock. And I had got used to having two of my brothers in the bed with me.

I lay there alone, listening to the far-away sounds of trains and trams. There were aeroplanes flying overhead — the war was on, and we were not too far as the crow flies from Speke Aerodrome, as it was then called. I cried myself to sleep.

* * *

On my first day in the class, the teacher started by introducing me to the rest of the pupils. She was surprised to discover that I could read Braille fluently, that I knew a lot of my prayers and was quite good with my arithmetic tables.

It was decided that I should move up two classes into Sister Joseph's class. Sister Joseph was the nun who had met me at the door the day before. She was actually the nun in charge of the boys' side of the school. There was also a girls' side, but I knew nothing of this at the time.

My homesickness stayed with me for weeks, particularly at nights. But even in the classroom during a dreary lesson I would be transported in my mind to 77A Queen's Road, Everton, playing on the 'ollers or sitting around the fire singing with my brothers and sisters.

I was a very quick learner. I could grasp things more quickly than my classmates. I have been asked whether my desire to be the best is a result of my blindness; whether I am trying to compensate, even overcompensate, for the loss of my sight. In some cases, this does happen, but not in mine, I think. After all, the other boys at both my schools were blind too. I was competing on level terms. I have always wanted to be first — second was never good enough for me. It's just the way I am.

We would be given an exercise to do in a certain time, and I would have it done in half the time. So my mind would wander. I became bored very easily and, to quote something constantly rammed down my throat by Sister Joseph, 'The Devil finds work for idle hands'.

Sister Joseph, who I later found out came from Swinford in Co. Mayo, was a very strict nun. She ruled by fear, and sometimes she was downright cruel and unjust. She was a very good teacher, but only for those pupils who were bright; she had no time for the 'slow learners'. She also knew nothing of the psychology of training blind children, understanding them, forming their characters and preparing them for the outside world.

I got many a severe beating from that nun, and quite often I wasn't in the wrong. You never answered back — you had no opportunity to put your side of the story. If she had decided that you were in the wrong, you were thoroughly beaten. She ruled with a rod of iron, which took the form of a bamboo cane, a cricket bat, or the nearest bit of wood to hand. Sometimes it was a sweeping brush and, on one occasion, a garden spade.

Many years later, I had the opportunity to meet Sister Joseph again and tell her exactly how I felt about my schooldays at St Vincent's. I was surprised when she told me that I had been one of her favourites.

* * *

About two weeks after my arrival at St Vincent's, on a Sunday afternoon after Benediction, I was called in from the playground and told I had visitors. I went into the corridor.

'Hello, Joe.'

To my utter joy, it was my sister Margaret who had come to see me. I couldn't believe it.

'Hello, Joe,' she repeated. Just hearing her voice made me burst into tears. I threw my arms around her, I couldn't let her go, I couldn't speak, I was choked. Eventually, I calmed down, we sat on the bench in the corridor, and Margaret told me all that was happening at home. She had come with one of her friends to see me.

'Mam couldn't come this time,' she told me, but she would come the next time.

Margaret had brought sweets and apples for me. She asked all about school. I said I wanted to leave and go home with her, that school was dreadful, the nuns hated me, all the boys jeered me about my Dublin accent, and the food was terrible.

She stayed for about an hour, then she hugged and kissed me, saying she would have to go. I was shattered, although she promised she would come and see me again in two weeks. This was all the visiting time allowed — once a fortnight.

'Be good, Joe,' she said, 'and learn well at school. Mam will come next time.' My mother did come to see me from time to time, but never as often as my sisters.

It took me several days to get over the visit. We were poor, dirty, and certainly not what you would call content, my parents weren't the best in the world, but there was a bond, particularly between us younger children. There was loyalty too, and I was something special to my family and they were extra special to me, even though we rarely spoke about it.

As time went on, I made many friends and became happier and less lonely. I did well in class, and outside the classroom I was always planning something or other to raise excitement — or mischief. I always had a gang around me. Sister Joseph called me 'The Magnet', saying that I could draw other boys towards me. Maybe because I came from a big family I felt comfortable in a group. I got into all sorts of trouble and took many a thrashing, and because I had a name for being a troublemaker, I often got blamed and punished for things I hadn't done.

One stupid rule that always got me into trouble was the one that forbade talking in the dormitory after the night prayer. If I couldn't sleep, I would carry on a whispered conversation with the lad in the next bed. In an effort to catch us breaking this rule, Sister Joseph would stand at the end of the dormitory, holding her rosary beads tightly in her hand so that they wouldn't rattle and give her presence away. Then she would creep down the dormitory to my bed, grab me by the hair, pull down the sheets, lift up my nightshirt and thrash me soundly. I would refuse to cry, although she hurt me, and this would enrage her even more. She would grind her teeth and give it all she had. There was a war of attrition between us. After nine years, I think it finished up as a draw.

As the end of my first term approached, I began to get really excited. I was going home, and to a new house. Margaret had told me this might happen, and on her last visit my mother had told me that the family had moved into a house not far from our original home. Our new address was 55 Spencer Street. We were still in Everton, but this house was in better condition than the previous one.

* * *

The last day of term finally arrived. I was going to be at home for six whole weeks. Everyone was delighted to see me when I got home, and they all remarked how well I looked. This was hardly surprising, as for three months I had been getting three meals a day, regular baths, cod liver oil every morning (which I thought was disgusting), and proper sleep.

My sister Sue said I talked 'real posh'. My Dublin accent was slowly disappearing thanks to 'How now brown cow' therapy at the elocution lessons I was taking.

It wasn't long before I was back into the swing of things in the street. We now even had a wireless. This was magic: there was an air-raid shelter beside the house, where we held 'concerts' most evenings. We soon made friends with the local kids and they made no fuss about my blindness — it was heaven.

Our new house was situated on the corner of Spencer Street and Belgrave Terrace, which was a small side street, containing two long air-raid shelters. I learned every inch of that area. I ran, skipped, jumped and even cycled up and down the terrace; I climbed up lamp posts and ran in and out of gardens. Of course, I got a few bumps and bangs, but all in the course of a day's fun, all part of the hazard of being a blind kid living and playing in a Liverpool slum. But it all had to come to an end. I had to go back to school, back to a life I'd already almost forgotten.

Returning to St Vincent's after my holidays was just like starting school all over again, except that this time, my mother came with me. I cried all the way on the tram and, by the time we finally got to the school, I was in hysterics. Sister Joseph took me gently by the hand, speaking soothingly while my mother was there, but as soon as my mother had gone the nun grabbed me by the shoulder and dragged me into her room where she shook me violently.

'Stop that silly crying at once, or I'll give you something to cry about.' At that particular moment, how I hated her.

I spent the next week crying myself to sleep at night and daydreaming about home during class.

* * *

When we resumed classes, I was told I would have to work hard at my religious studies this term, as I was to make my first Holy Communion.

Studying was no problem to me: I had arrived at St Vincent's knowing all the prayers said by Catholic children. I did have to relearn the catechism, however, as the words of the English catechism were different from those of the Irish one. Of course, everything was learned parrot fashion — we repeated everything the nun said and kept it in our heads.

We prayed all together and all the time. There were morning prayers, said when the nun came into the dormitory and clapped her hands to wake us all up; there was Grace before and after breakfast; there were prayers before, during and after Morning Assembly; prayers before the day's work in the classroom; the Angelus at twelve o'clock; Grace before and after dinner; prayers before resumption of afternoon class; Angelus at six o'clock; Grace before and after tea; rosary and trimmings at seven in the chapel; evening prayers recited in the recreation room before going up to the dormitory; and finally, night prayers, said sitting up in bed before the nun put the light out. We needed lights both for the nuns and for those boys who were not totally blind but were partially sighted (the term used in those days for the current 'visual impairment').

Among the things I did have to learn when I joined the school were the Latin prayers and hymns. I didn't know what they were about, so I just listened to the boy next to me and repeated what I thought he was saying or singing.

Benediction, which took place at least three times during the week, was always a great puzzle to me. We would sing three hymns in Latin while the thurible was swung, full of smelly incense which made my eyes water. We sang the *Adoramus in Aeturnum* at the end of the Benediction. This contains the *Gloria Patri*, and when we came to the words '*Secut erat in Precepio*', for a long time I sang, 'See the parrot in the GPO'. I really thought those were the words.

My Communion day was to be on the feast of Christ the King, the last Sunday in October. There was only myself and another boy called Richard making our Communion, and the day before that we were to make our First Confession. Confessions were held every Saturday morning at eleven o'clock, and every boy was made to go to confession every week. On the momentous day we all filed into the chapel and I was designated to be the first to go.

As I knelt there waiting for the priest to arrive, my heart was pounding. Richard knelt beside me.

'I haven't done any sins,' I whispered.

'Make them up,' he suggested.

Then I had a brainwave. I would take the Ten Commandments, go through them one by one, and tell the priest I had broken them all.

The priest arrived and I made my way to the confessional. I could smell him on the other side of the mesh screen. He smoked a pipe — I could smell it on his clothes. And he had had soup before he came to the chapel — I could smell his breath.

'Bless me, Father, for I have sinned,' I began. 'I have worshipped false Gods, I have taken the Lord's name in vain, I have not kept holy the Sabbath day.' So far it was easy. 'I have not honoured my father and mother —' Now I had a problem. The fifth commandment said, 'Thou shalt not kill'. What should I tell him? Then I had an idea: 'I killed a wasp on Thursday, I have committed adultery —'

'Wait a minute, child,' the priest interrupted my flow. 'How old are you?'

'Seven, Father.'

'Well, don't make up your sins in future. Say one Hail Mary for your penance and ask the nuns to give you instructions in examining your conscience.' I decided not to tell him that I didn't know what this meant.

As I left the confessional, Richard passed me.

'Don't be making them up — he's tumbled to it,' I whispered.

* * *

My First Communion the following morning was an occasion of great excitement in the school, particularly among the nuns. I was dressed in a little white suit, and knelt with Richard in the front kneeler. The school choir sang the appropriate hymns and, at the Communion itself, Sister Joseph led me to the altar rails.

After Communion, I said a prayer to myself and asked the Baby Jesus to let my mother come and visit me today.

After Mass, all the nuns hugged me and I was given sweets and bars of chocolate. One nun actually gave me a holy picture, though I don't know how she thought I was going to see it.

'It's to hang over your bed,' she said.

We had a party at lunchtime, and still I waited. After Benediction in the afternoon, I began to get excited. Someone *should* come from home today — after all it was Sunday and the day for visiting. Four o'clock came, then five o'clock, but when the tea bell ran at six, I knew that no one was coming to visit me on my First Communion day. Richard's parents had come to see him and had taken a photograph of both of us, and they lived in Preston, which was much further away than Everton.

I made excuses when the other boys asked me why my parents hadn't come.

'Mam has a lot to do at home with such a big family'; 'My Dad is away'; 'My big sister has to look after the baby' — I lied again and again.

That night, I really tried hard not to cry, but tears flowed onto my pillow. I felt that those I loved most in the world had let me down again.

I didn't think an awful lot of Baby Jesus either. Even He hadn't helped me.

~ Four ~

The next five years at St Vincent's were a mixture of good and bad for me. Academically, I blossomed, always being the star pupil because of my quick imagination. Learning was easy: when the rest of the class was struggling with long division, I would have finished and be doodling away at something else. Often, I would be writing poetry for my own amusement. My first finished poem was about my grandmother, although both grandmothers were long since dead. This poem was based on my paternal grandmother, not the alcoholic one.

Sister Joseph caught me writing the poem into a notebook and confiscated it. Afterwards, she took me aside and complimented me on it, encouraging me to write more — but not in arithmetic class. As I got older and my work improved, Sister Joseph mellowed towards me. I suppose she felt I was doing her credit.

At that time, there was great competition in Braille reading between the various schools for the blind in England. St Vincent's was the only Roman Catholic school for the blind in the country, but there were several other schools for blind children. One was in Manchester, and there was a girls' school, in Chorleywood in the south.

Every year, the National Library for the Blind would organise an inter-school reading competition, one in the north of England and, later in the year, one in London. Each school would enter a team of three students in different age groups, and the winners would receive a silver cup, which they would keep until the following year.

The competitions lasted all day. In the morning we would have to read to one of the adjudicators in a small booth, and if we passed that test, we would have to read in the afternoon, on a stage in front of a large audience. We would have to read a poem or a passage of prose 'cold' — a sort of sight-reading, if you could call it that.

When I was ten years old, Sister Joseph decided that my Braille reading was good enough for me to be entered in the team for the under-sixteen class for the Braille reading competition in Manchester. I thought the whole thing was a terrible bore. I loved reading and read everything I could get my hands on. I was reading all the time — but for my own pleasure. Reading as a sport or game has always seemed stupid to me.

We headed off for Manchester, and Sister Joseph told me not to be upset if I didn't get anywhere in the competition as I was very young for the class I was in. There would be lots of chances in the years to come.

In the morning session, I went into the booth to read for the adjudicator, only to discover when I placed my hand on the book that the piece I had to read was taken from *Treasure Island*. I happened to be reading this book in my spare time, so the test couldn't have been easier. I flew through it and, to everybody's surprise except mine, I was in the final in the afternoon — the only boy from St Vincent's to make it through.

In the afternoon session, all the competitors were kept in a room a long way from the auditorium so that we couldn't hear what was being read. Then, when our turn came, we would have to read to the judges and the packed auditorium, from an unseen passage. We would be judged on our interpretation of the passage, our speed, delivery and so on.

That afternoon, I wasn't paying much attention to what was going on as I was busy finding out from the other kids what life was like at their school. Suddenly my name was called and an usher brought me up on stage.

'And now we have Joseph Bollard, representing St Vincent's School for the Blind in Liverpool,' said the announcer.

I sat down at the table, placed my hand on the page I was to read and discovered that it was a poem I knew by heart — 'Tartary' by Walter de la Mare. The judges didn't know I knew it and I gave it all I had. Although I didn't have to worry about reading it, I ran my fingers over the page as I recited it with the necessary expression. The applause was tremendous. Naturally I won the cup and there was great celebration in the school. I also got a guinea and a box of chocolates from the judges — which meant more to me than a silly silver cup.

I wasn't as lucky as that again, but I won that cup five years in a row. I have always been an avid reader, so I got plenty of practice at reading in Braille.

* * *

Soon after I arrived at St Vincent's, an elocution teacher was engaged to help the pupils to improve their speech and get rid of their various accents. It was like the Tower of Babel: there were children who came from Yorkshire, Lancashire, Newcastle upon Tyne, Birmingham, London, Portsmouth and parts of Wales, while my accent was a mixture of Dublin and Scouse. The good nuns tried their best to get rid of our accents — they saw a definite need for elocution lessons.

The new teacher introduced us to acting, and our first attempt was a passion play for Easter. I never quite got hold of the plot, but I know I was Judas Iscariot. Shortly before the play was due to go on at the end-of-term concert, the priest came to visit our class for the weekly catechism test. He was curious about the forthcoming play.

'Well, Joseph, and what part are you playing?'

'Please Father, I'm acting Judas the Scallywag who sells Jesus for thirty pieces of silver paper and then Jesus is prophesied on the cross by the dirty Jews,' I innocently replied.

At the end of the year, we put on a Nativity play and, being the only Joseph in the class, I was cast as St Joseph.

'Alec, you can be the Virgin Mary.'

'Please Miss, what's a virgin?'

'Never mind, Bollard, you'll learn when you're older.'

'Alec's too fat to be a virgin, Miss,' said somebody better informed than I. Alec was huge and we teased him something terrible about it.

As Joseph was a carpenter, I was given a hammer to carry as a mark of my trade. During the play, one of the shepherds accidentally poked me in the eye. I thought he'd done it on purpose, so I smote him on the knee with my hammer; he lashed out at me but unfortunately hit one of the angels by mistake. A general fracas ensued. Sister Joseph bounded onto the stage, cane whirling. 'Joseph Bollard, you are the cause of this trouble! There'll be no party for you tonight.'

Later she relented, and I was allowed to join the others at the end-of-term party.

Our next production was a version of *The Three Musketeers*, and yet again I was in trouble. I never took acting seriously, often forgot my lines and would ad lib to the horror of the teacher. At one point in the play I was supposed to say, 'Hark, I hear a pistol shot! Oh, see, I am shot!' Instead it came out as 'Hark, I hear a shostle pit — oh no, I mean a shistle pot - oh, shit, I'm shot!'

The cast got a fit of the giggles and no one could speak, the giggling spread to the audience, and eventually the whole school hall was echoing with hysterical laughter. The curtain was brought down, and I was severely reprimanded, as they say in the courts, and warned about my future conduct in the drama class.

Nothing disastrous happened when we did *A Christmas Carol,* I am glad to say, as I love Dickens. It was a different story when we did Shakespeare's *Henry V* though. How I hated that man. I was a page, bringing a message from the French king to King Henry. I had to wear silly tights and as I was putting them on, my shoe caught in them and tore a hole in the backside. This was just before my entrance, so there was nothing to do but go on and hope nobody would notice.

I made my entrance to a packed hall filled with teachers, parents (not mine, they never came to our plays) and friends. I knelt before King Henry and began my lines. Suddenly, a child's voice from the audience interrupted my speech. 'Hey Ma, I can see his bum!'

I dried up — couldn't remember a word. It was ad lib time again: 'My Lord King, I must leave in a hurry forsooth. My garb doth not become me. Once more into my breeches, dear friends.' Old Bill Shakespeare would have been proud of me, but not so our drama teacher who tore strips off me for making a mockery of the 'Immortal Bard'!

* * *

From my early days at St Vincent's, I was very interested in sport, especially soccer and cricket. Although blind, we boys devised our own versions of these games. When we played soccer, we put peas inside the football so that we could hear it as it travelled along. You could get quite skilful at this, and could judge the speed of the ball, particularly if it was rolling along the ground or bouncing.

We played in a small field which ran alongside the main body of the school and behind the chapel. It was because of the proximity of the field to the chapel that I had another encounter with the Blessed Virgin — or at least with her statue.

This field was known as the 'Cabbage Plot' for reasons unknown, and at the end of it and beside the chapel was a small grotto with a statue of the Blessed Virgin, this time without the child Jesus. One day we were having a five-a-side soccer game, with the grotto behind one of the goals. I was playing on the wing. We were attacking. I heard the ball bounce in front of me, and one of my partially sighted team-mates shouted, 'It's yours, Bollard!' I caught the ball beautifully on the half volley, it flew over the bar, travelled onwards and upwards, then, smack, it hit the statue of the Blessed Virgin.

There was a dull thud and we all rushed round behind the goal to see what had happened. There we found it — the head of the Virgin lying at the foot of the statue. It took two of us to pick it up. We examined it and found that it had snapped cleanly off.

'Put it back on again, on top, and leave it there. We'll say nothing about it,' I instructed.

Three days later we had a storm and the following morning at Assembly Sister Joseph informed us that the wind had been so strong that it had blown off the head of the Blessed Virgin in the grotto. It was repaired some time later, but I'm sure Our Blessed Lady had a heavenly giggle over that one.

* * *

When I was eleven years old, I was moved into the senior class, and it was there that I met Mrs Bold for the first time.

Now here was a real dragon of a teacher. She was English to the core and patriotic in the extreme. We had to listen to Winston Churchill every time he was on the wireless, and to learn parts of his speeches by heart. We had to learn English patriotic songs — 'There'll Always be an England', 'Rule Britannia', 'Hearts of Oak', 'Land of Hope and Glory', and even the second verse of 'God Save the King', which nobody ever sang. She never used corporal punishment, but her shout could have wakened the dead, and she put the fear of God into her pupils.

While I was in her class, I improved tremendously at schoolwork, perhaps because I was terrified of her. She did, however, approve of my love of poetry and encouraged me to read more. But oh Lord! I never hear Winston Churchill's name, even to this day, without thinking of her.

* * *

One of my best friends at St Vincent's was Bobby Bell. Bob came from Jarrow, up near Newcastle upon Tyne. He always kept his Geordie accent, and in fact I picked up some of it from him and would use Geordie expressions at times. Like me, he came from a very large family. He wasn't totally blind, but as a child he had developed rickets and had suffered from malnutrition so severe that it had caused his sight to deteriorate. He was a beanpole of a boy, and wore callipers on his legs to help him walk. Bob and I had great times together — he had the heartiest laugh I have ever heard.

One day, Bob and I went off to the orchard to steal apples. He would use what little sight he had to tell me where the apples were and on what tree, and I would climb up and throw them down to him. The plan worked for a while — we had gathered quite a few apples in a paper bag and I was climbing a very large tree with the best apples up near the top. Then it happened: the branch I was standing on broke, I came crashing down and hit the ground with a bump, falling on my head.

I must have been knocked unconscious for a little while, as when I came around, Bob was smacking my face and shouting, 'Wake up, you stupid clot!'

I finally got myself together, only to discover that I couldn't put my foot on the ground — I couldn't walk. We were at the far end of the field and a good way from the playground. Bob, who was as skinny as a rake and certainly not very strong, suddenly gritted his teeth, picked me up, and carried me all the way back to the school. He staggered, stumbled and groped his way along with the sweat pouring off him. We got as far as the school buildings, and then he collapsed. I managed to hobble inside and bring him a drink of water from the washroom. He sat there, gasping for breath, while I was crying with the pain of my ankle, which had swollen up like a football.

Suddenly I heard a rustling noise.

'What's that?' I asked.

'It's the bag of apples,' said Bob. 'You didn't think I was going to leave those little beauties behind, did you?' He had carried me and the big bag of apples all the way across a wide field, and he hardly able to walk himself.

Later, I reported my ankle to the nun in charge of the dispensary and told her I'd fallen down the steps outside the toilets. Bob and I had a great time eating the apples for the next week, and we told nobody about our experience. We got into many scrapes at St Vincent's and we remained firm buddies until his death, as a result of a heart condition, in the mid-1960s. Bob's hearty laugh will always stay in my memory.

My other good friend at school was Alf or, to give him his full name, Alfredo Adanez. His parents were Spanish and he came from Liverpool. Alf and Bob were as different as chalk from cheese. Alf was extremely intelligent and helped me a great deal with my studies. He encouraged me to read and recommended many books to me. He sat beside me in the classroom and we were always getting told off for whispering to each other. He knew I was clever and would tell me off for wasting time playing silly games instead of studying.

He would say, 'You shouldn't be messing about, Joe. You have more brains than most of us and you should use them.' Later on, like me, he got a scholarship to Worcester College for the Blind, but unlike me, he attended that college and went on to get a degree in Social Science at Liverpool University in days when few blind people did that.

When Alf left college, he and I corresponded regularly, and

when I was in England we used to meet. He didn't have a very happy life, and died of cancer at the age of forty-two.

* * *

When I was twelve years old, something wonderful happened to me. It was the policy of the school that every pupil should study music for a year and then, if he showed any promise, he was encouraged to continue his studies.

I remember every moment of my first music lesson. I went into the music room and met Miss Connor. She was a gentle lady who took my hand and led me to the piano, where she sat me down, and told me to run my hands over the keyboard and tell her what I felt. I told her that there were flat pieces at the front and raised-up, narrow pieces behind them. The raised-up pieces were placed in groups of two three — two three. She told me the raised-up narrow pieces were black and the flat pieces were white. I pressed a key and, oh, what a wonderful sound! I took to music like a duck to water. Completely smitten, I told myself, 'It's music for me.' I was to have music lessons twice a week and practise every evening.

That night, I dreamt of the piano, of music and of Miss Connor. I'd fallen in love with all three. Miss Connor was the first woman I'd fallen in love with — I thought she was gorgeous, with her soft voice and her lovely musky scent. A whole new world was opening for me. I was on cloud nine.

My love of music is with me still. My love for Miss Connor lasted all of three weeks, ending when she cracked me over the knuckles for allowing my wrists to drop and for not practising what I'd been taught. I'd started to use my ear to pick up popular songs of the day, but we were strictly forbidden to 'pick up'. Somebody had heard me trying to play 'Swanee River' during my practice and had reported me to Miss Connor.

It didn't stop me experimenting. I would pick up variations on popular songs, and play and sing, having very little idea of their meaning.

Bewitched again, beguiled again
My girlfriend's expecting a child again...

A sharp blow on the ear would silence me.

I began to play the piano quite well. Of course, it wasn't sufficient for me to play by ear, I had to learn to read Braille music. Braille, as we know, is a system of writing and printing to enable blind people to read, using their fingers. It's complicated and takes a good deal of learning and, in fact, only about 10 per cent of blind people in Ireland actually read Braille. Braille music is even more complicated, and there are very few blind musicians in Ireland who read it. Unlike printed music, Braille music doesn't consist of five lines and four spaces, but uses Braille letters as notes. It makes use of various other Braille symbols for fingering, expressions, octave signs, time signatures and key signatures.

Obviously, it's not possible to play and read Braille music at the same time. You have to read ahead a couple of bars, remember what you have read, and play it. It's an advantage in learning Braille, both words and music, if you have had to do so from a young age as I did. It may be compared with learning another language, which is always easier for a child than an adult. Nowadays, the computer has come to the fore as an aid to blind musicians. With a computer, it is possible to print out a score. But computers hadn't been invented then.

I studied music with Miss Connor until I was fourteen years old, when she retired and I started to learn with Alan Mapson, who was himself blind.

For me, music was a marvellous new experience. I passed my first music exam with distinction, and the second, and the third. The school was thrilled with my performance and, what's more, I was enjoying it. My love for music has never altered: music was my life and still is. Along with learning to play the piano, I was taught to play the organ, or harmonium to be exact, and was required to play for Benediction three times a week. The harmonium was in the gallery over the chapel and I was given the gallery key to keep in my locker so that I could practise three times a week.

It was because I had this key that the Great Clock Robbery took place. Bob and I planned this operation in great detail beforehand. The chapel clock hung from the gallery at the back of the chapel and struck the hour and half hour with a loud DONG. One summer's night, Bob and I crept along the corridor leading to the gallery. There would be nobody in the chapel at this time — it was almost midnight. I opened the gallery door with the key (it squeaked so I had to take it easy). No problem so far. We didn't need lights. I leaned far over the gallery rail, Bob holding my ankles. I reached for the clock, found it and whispered, 'Okay Bob, lift.'

The clock weighed much more than I expected. Bob heaved, I lifted and almost dropped it down into the chapel, but we got it up. We carried it between us back along the corridor, down the side stairs, and as I leaned down to unbolt the side door to the back of the school, the stupid clock struck *twelve*. It echoed along the corridors, seemingly for ever. We froze, listening. It sounded like Big Ben. For an age we waited to be discovered but nobody came. We brought the clock around to the back of the boiler-house, crept back through the door, bolted it behind us and sneaked back to the dormitory. We'd done it.

It is hard to believe, but it was two days before that clock was missed! At Assembly, Sister Joseph was at her best. She said that she knew who had taken the clock and she would wait for them to come forward and confess. Until then, all privileges would be stopped: no swimming, no late nights at the weekend, no visits to the woods for nature walks. Bob and I stayed mum. Three days later, Harrison, the school handyman, was cleaning behind the boiler-house and discovered the clock. There was no serious damage done to it and nobody ever knew who had taken it.

* * *

Sex was never discussed at St Vincent's — we had no idea of the facts of life. Any information we got was picked up from other boys, from dirty jokes, from hearsay and from looking up words we overheard in the dictionary. This was partly the way things were in these days, but also partly I'm sure because there was a tendency to treat people with disabilities as if they had no sexual feelings.

I first became aware of my sexuality when I was ten years old. We had bath nights on Thursdays. This event was always overseen by a member of the staff. It always seemed to me that we were rushed in and rushed out as quickly as possible — no hanging around.

One Thursday night I was drying myself and I noticed that when drying between my legs it felt rather odd — nice, but odd. I kept rubbing the towel against myself and felt that my willy was getting harder and standing up for itself. I still kept rubbing with a towel. I was really enjoying this, when suddenly I felt very strange and liquid came gushing out of my willy. Oh Lord, I'm bleeding, I thought, thoroughly alarmed. Not being able to see what was coming out, I thought it was blood and that I had done something dreadful to myself. I wiped myself down and told nobody what had happened.

A short time afterwards when lying in bed, I felt it getting hard again, but this time I used my hand, and again I thought I was bleeding. I confided in Alf, and he laughed at me and told me I was committing a dreadful mortal sin. It wasn't blood, he said. He wasn't quite sure what it was but I would have to confess it when I went to confession.

'You'll have to tell the priest you committed the sin of adultery — it's against the sixth commandment,' he told me.

So *that's* what committing adultery means, I thought.

When I told the priest in confession about my sin, he gave me six Our Fathers and six Hail Marys and told me not to do it again. It wasn't adultery, he informed me, but it was a grave sin. I continued in ignorance as before.

As for girls, I loved being with them and got a great buzz when I was with a girl. I was the life and soul of mixed parties and used to show off terribly. Until I was thirteen, the two sections of the school — boys and girls — only met for meals in the refectory and for Mass in the chapel. Then the school was reorganised. The partially sighted boys and girls were to be together in class, as were the totally blind pupils. We were not to mix at recreation.

Now I started meeting girls — boy, this was great! I began to look forward to class with a new zest. I was sweet on one particular girl, Mary, and we became great friends. I used to bring her sweets, or maybe an orange or a bar of chocolate. We were about the same age and I thought she was wonderful. Then one day we arranged to meet secretly after school.

This was the plan. I went to bed in the dormitory as usual at half past eight, and at nine o'clock I got up, took my clothes into the loo, got dressed there, got out through the window and groped for the drainpipe that ran down the wall. I slid down quietly to the grass below, made my way around the back of the building, quietly across the playground, slipped behind the hedge at the top end and met her there. I left the loo door locked, and the plan worked perfectly. We sat for about an hour, chatting about this and that, holding hands, with the odd cuddle and a few kisses.

Then I said goodnight and made my way back. This was more nerve-racking than getting out. I regained the shelter of the wall, and counted the drainpipes — one, two, three — then shinned up the fourth one, hoping to God I hadn't been missed. All was well: the loo door was still locked. I got undressed and crept back to bed.

I repeated this adventure many times and I was never caught. We used to go to the chapel for the rosary at seven o'clock, and if Mary coughed at the second mystery, it meant that she wouldn't be able to meet me that night.

One night, my lack of knowledge of female matters caused me great embarrassment. She seemed sort of quiet, maybe a bit uneasy. At last she said, 'I've something to tell you.'

'What is it?' I asked.

'I got my monthly for the first time today.'

I hadn't a clue what she was talking about but I didn't want to let her know that — I thought it must be a magazine.

'Did you enjoy it?' I stupidly asked, and made it worse by adding, 'Will you bother getting it again?'

'Joe Bollard, you make a joke out of everything,' she said, slapping me on the shoulder.

I was thirteen years old, but I honestly didn't know what she meant, and didn't find out for another three years.

* * *

This ignorance was bad, but worse was to come. A year later, I had a dreadful experience, made far worse by my ignorance.

Every month, the doctor would visit the school and examine us from head to toe. This was always a great source of fun and we would swap stories as to what he did or said to us. Of course, we went through the well-known routine of dropping trousers and coughing. We were never told why this was done, but we would joke about it among ourselves.

One morning after breakfast, the little nun who was in charge of the dispensary and all things medical called me to one side and told me that I was going into hospital.

'What for, Sister?' I asked.

'You're going to be circumcised,' she said. I had no idea what she meant. Somehow I imagined it was something to do with my eyes — 'circums-eyes'. Then I remembered that we'd learned in Scripture that Jesus was circumcised. Perhaps it was something to do with religion.

The following morning, I went to the local hospital with this little nun. I was led into a cubicle and told to strip and wait. The nun still didn't tell me what was going to happen to me, just left me there. I waited, still wondering if they were going to do something to my eyes. Eventually a doctor arrived. Imagine my shock and surprise when he grabbed my willy and began to examine it.

'Hey, what are you doing?' I yelled.

'Stop that nonsense, you're going to be circumcised.'

Oh Lord, I thought, they're going to chop off my willy.

The next morning, I was taken down to the operating theatre, still not knowing what was going to happen to me. I asked, and was again told, 'You're going to be circumcised.' I was fourteen years old, but nobody would tell me what circumcised meant.

When I woke up after the operation, oh Jesus, the pain! And was I sick? When I tried to investigate the damage, my hands met dressings and bandages. More scared than ever, I asked the nurse what had happened to me.

'You've been circumcised,' she said. Still no explanation.

At last I found out from the doctor what they'd done to me.

'It should have been done when you were a baby,' he said severely. I remember thinking that if they'd spent more time dealing with my willy and less messing around with my eyes, things might have been different. But then, maybe they would have severed that nerve instead....

I was kept in hospital for about a week, and when I left I was given long instructions about taking lots of hot baths, and was given dressings to put on the wound.

When I returned to the school, the little nun in charge of the dispensary immediately took me under her wing. She told me to report to the dispensary each morning for dressing.

I did as she said and on the first morning she told me to drop my trousers. Fit, healthy fourteen-year-old lad that I was, as she fingered my most treasured possession I began to have an erection, and it was quite sizeable. I started to worry about what might happen, but the nun kept reassuring me: 'It's all right, child, don't worry, it's not a sin.'

I wasn't worried about the sin of it, and still she kept wrapping this bandage around my willy, fingering it as she did so. I didn't know what to do. I tried to move away, but she just pulled me back towards her. That did it. It happened, just as I feared it would. Wham! An ejaculation to beat all ejaculations. I was mortified.

'Don't worry, Joseph,' she said. 'You couldn't help it. It's nature taking its course and, as I've said, it's no sin.'

It was all over the place: on her, on me, on the floor — what a mess. That was it.

'Sister,' I said. 'I'll do my own dressing in future. I know what to do.'

'All right, Joseph, but you mustn't worry. It's all part of growing up.' She was a lovely little nun and I know she was only trying to help me: she thought that being blind I wouldn't be able to manage the dressing. But oh why didn't somebody explain to me what was happening?

From then on, I looked after my own willy.

Still, I suppose there aren't too many men who can say that they were helped to achieve an orgasm by a nun!

Later, the little nun left the order and got married.

~ Five ~

One afternoon when I was fourteen, Sister Joseph sent for Alf and me and told us that we were going to sit for the scholarship for Worcester College at the end of term. We would have to work hard, she said.

We set to work to study and when we finally sat the exam, I found it quite easy. After some weeks of waiting, we were called into Sister Joseph's office, and I was surprised and delighted to find that my mother was there, along with Alf's mum. We were given the good news that we had got the scholarship, and I had got the highest marks in the exam. Great, I thought, thrilled that I was going to be able to go to college. Sister Joseph gave us cakes and lemonade and we sat and chatted about the future. I said I wanted to study music and physiotherapy. I knew I'd have to work hard and was looking forward to it.

Then my mother asked, 'What nuns are running that college, Sister?'

'There are no nuns, Mrs Bollard. It's not a Catholic school,' Sister Joseph replied.

'Not a Catholic school? Then how do the Catholic boys get to Mass?'

'There are no provisions made for the Catholic boys to attend Mass,' stated Sister Joseph.

I couldn't believe what I was hearing. I really thought that they were pretending, just to tease me. When I realised that they were serious, I was devastated.

It was some time before I discovered that my parents had been deceived — and the reason for it. The nuns were proud of my achievements: my high marks in the scholarships, my honours in music exams and, above all, that silver cup for Braille reading that I'd won year after year. I was a sort of trophy myself, a feather in the cap of the school and, come hell or high water, they were determined to keep me there.

In much the same way, boys who were brilliant at Rugby but academically rather thick were often kept on at university so that they could win matches for their colleges. Sometimes their fees were waived.

I was told that I would be 'allowed' to remain at St Vincent's until I was sixteen, studying reading and music — and winning further awards for the nuns. After that, the future looked bleak. I was to be sent to the Catholic Blind Asylum to train as a mat maker. I was to be deprived of the education that I had earned.

The last thing I wanted to do was to tear my hands to bits making doormats, but nobody listened to my arguments. My mother remained adamant, refusing to talk about it and telling the rest of the family, 'Joe doesn't want to go to college.' She was simply too uneducated, too much in awe of authority and too easily swayed by the nuns to question them. My father backed out of the discussion, saying that he was only a builder's labourer and wouldn't be able to afford the money I'd need to 'keep up with the rest of the college boys'. 'You'd need a lot of pocket money there, Joe,' he said.

For two years I marked time, often out of the classroom, practising the piano, reading, spending time on the farm in summer, and looking after some of the youngest boys. I felt angry, resentful and disappointed and was only happy when I was at home with my brothers and sisters. I missed Alf dreadfully, as I'd thought he'd write to me, but no letters came. Years later, I met him when he was at university and he asked, 'Why didn't you answer my letters?'

'What letters?' I said. Alf told me that he'd written every fortnight in Braille. The nuns had withheld all his letters because if I'd read them I'd soon have discovered that provisions *were* made for Catholic boys to attend Mass. There were only six of them and they were taken by taxi.

The mat shop which I was to attend was, I need hardly say, run by nuns.

* * *

Nowadays there are many courses for blind and visually impaired people dealing with everyday situations. There are rehabilitation courses, daily-living skills courses, mobility courses and others, which help us to cope with the stresses and strains of being blind in a seeing society.

However, when I left St Vincent's, I found myself turfed out into the seeing world with no advice as to how to cope. I was just given a white stick — an ordinary walking stick with a curved handle (at that time we didn't have the long white canes that can be folded up), and no advice as to how to use it.

Today, thank God, mobility instruction explains the correct way to use a white cane — and there is a correct way. A great deal of research has been undertaken to help us overcome the problem of getting around, because mobility is one of the biggest problems that confront blind people today. It doesn't matter whether you have been blind from birth or have just become newly blind, getting from A to B can cause horrendous problems if you can't see.

Many blind people have the ability to feel the closeness of an object. It can only be described as feeling the presence of an object through 'facial perception'. If I am walking along a street with nothing beside me and I come across a lamp post on my right-hand side, suddenly the air pressure changes. I can feel that lamp post through the surface down the right side of my face. I cannot tell what the object is — it might be a lamp post, a tree or even a person standing still at the side of the pavement, but I can feel it. Some years ago, the Russians were trying to develop this theory to discover whether it might be possible for a totally blind person to distinguish objects through 'facial perception'. I don't know how far they got in their experiments.

Mind you, you can still bump your nose. Facial perception only works on the side of your face.

There is also what I call the 'bat syndrome' because it is used by bats as they fly around in the dark. They emit a high-pitched squeak which rebounds off objects in close proximity. They can then judge the distance of the object and avoid it. If I am close to an object, I can click my fingers and the echo bounces back to me. I can usually judge the distance but it needs working on. A lot of blind people find it hard to use this method of object finding, and it works better out of doors in a quiet area. A sophisticated version of the bat syndrome used to be used by warships to detect enemy ships, and was called 'sonar'. It was replaced by the more efficient radar.

My first venture out with my newly acquired white stick took place on a Monday evening in September 1951. As the song from *Gigi* says, 'I remember it well.'

I wanted to make my way from the workshop in Brunswick Road to my home in Spencer Street, a distance of a mile or so. I knew the area quite well, which helped a great deal. Holding the white stick in my left hand, I took a few hesitant steps forward as I left the building, my heart pounding. I was terrified. I tried to keep as close to the wall on my left as possible. When I was holding onto somebody's arm, I could move fast and was quick on my feet, but when left to myself in a strange environment it was a different story.

I sort of groped my way up Brunswick Road, and when I came to a crossing, I just stood rigid. A woman came and took me over to the other side — fine, I thought, I'm making some headway. Suddenly, my stick got caught in a metal grille covering a cellar. I tried to wrestle it free — no joy. I started to panic. The more I pulled, the more it stuck. Eventually, a young lad who was laughing at my predicament managed to prise the stick free of the grille.

I shuffled slowly along Everton Road, smelling my way past the sauce factory, the nose being another useful navigational aid for blind people. I went sprawling over a parked motor bike outside the Red Triangle Club, then I stepped in some dog mess, skidded and almost fell on my backside.

Further along the road, I knew there was a tram stop. As I approached the spot where I thought it should be, I felt a presence. 'Ah, the tram stop, nearly there,' I told myself, and I lashed out with the stick, expecting to hear a clank as it hit the metal stop. Imagine my horror when, instead of a clank, I felt a dead thud. Then an irate male voice shouted, 'If you do that again, I'll shove that stick up your arse!'

As I reached the corner of Spencer Street, I had to cross to the other side of the road. I listened carefully: nothing coming, over we go. Then I heard a shout, 'Look out!'

Crash! I hadn't heard the bike and we both finished up on the road. I had a cut over my left eye, and the cyclist was rubbing his arm. 'You bloody fool, you should have someone with you who can see — you're dangerous out on your own.' I hadn't thought of listening for traffic other than cars.

When I eventually got home, my mother, who never molly-coddled me, was quite blasé about the whole episode. 'Just a part of learning how to get around on your own,' she said.

With a large sticking plaster over my eye at the time, I can't say I agreed with her.

* * *

While some people are perfectly safe with the cane alone, I never became really good at getting around with either the stick or even the long white cane.

Once during my early efforts at mobility, I was standing at the side of the road outside a shop. Feeling a presence, I plucked up courage, and said, 'Excuse me, I wonder if you could take me across the road, please?' There was no reply so I asked again, thinking that in the traffic my plea had not been heard. Still no reply, so I asked a third time, in a louder voice.

From behind me a young lad's voice shouted, 'Hey, Mister, you're talking to a horse.' There was a horse and cart parked outside the shop. I soon learned to take nothing for granted.

Another day, I bumped into a ladder, at the top of which was perched a window cleaner with bucket and water — window cleaner, me, ladder and aforementioned bucket of water finished up tangled in a struggling mess on the pavement. He shouted and cursed, I apologised, while passers-by were breaking their hearts laughing. A Liverpool wag shouted, 'You certainly made a splash that time, Joe Bollard!'

It was around that time that I began to be aware of the attitude of many people towards blindness. I considered it — as I still do — a bloody nuisance. In my early teens, I began to notice people saying, 'Ah, will you look at the poor blind boy,

God love him!' It never occurred to them that my ears were in perfect working order.

That pitying note, which I and others like me learn to dread, crept into their voices. When I grew older and was more on my own, I had to listen to it all the time, the word 'poor' always there — 'There goes a poor blind man, God help him!' and that curious saying, 'A terrible thing, the sight.' I suppose they knew what they meant. I didn't want to know.

~ Six ~

In September 1951, I began my training as a mat maker at the Catholic Blind Asylum. Two years later, the name was changed to the Catholic Blind Institute. I think the change was made to improve the image of the place, but to my mind it didn't work: it was still a cross between a Dickensian workhouse and an old county home, although not quite as bad as either.

It had been built in the early 1900s on Brunswick Road, and had a hateful atmosphere of poverty, dreariness and downright depression. It was run by the Sisters of Charity and I know they did their best with the help of the welfare authority, but it should never have been allowed to exist. It was a dreadful hole.

There were six of us in the male section and we were known as trainees. Two of us trained in the mat shop and the other four trained in the basket shop. My training in the mat shop was to last for three years. Although the building was only about a mile from my home, I was allowed home only at the weekends. I used to sneak home in the evenings after tea, but I had to be back again by ten o'clock.

There was also a female section to this establishment, where a number of blind and visually impaired girls were trained as knitting machinists. They were not boarders in the building, but travelled out to West Derby each evening to their residence, and back again in the morning. Officially we never came in contact with them.

The place was always referred to as 'Brunswick Road' when it was being spoken about. 'Do you work at Brunswick Road?' people would ask when I met them. I cannot adequately express my loathing for it. I suppose it wasn't anybody's fault — they all thought they were doing the right thing for me, giving me a chance to make a life for myself as a mat maker. But I wanted to be a musician — to hell with mats!

There were, however, two people who had a great influence on me and the shaping of my character during those years at Brunswick Road. The first was Larry Doyle, my boss in the mat shop, whose job was to train me in the 'art' of producing good doormats. He must have seen some potential in me, as he took me under his wing and as we worked he would talk, and not only about mats. He would instruct me about everyday matters, especially concerning blind people and blindness.

He was partially sighted himself and could discuss and instruct on any subject I brought up. He didn't stay in the building overnight, but went home to his wife and two children at half past six every evening. He would come in early next morning and give me a full description of the previous evening's television programmes. Television was only just coming into its own in Liverpool at the time, and we didn't have one in our house until 1965, but through Larry Doyle I became *au fait* with all the television programmes of the day.

Larry was a non-smoking, non-drinking, non-swearing person and he had no time for dirty jokes. He had a hearty laugh and would show his approval of anything I did by slapping me hard on the back. 'Well done, young Bollard, we'll make something of you yet,' he would say.

He shared my love of classical music and would give me records of symphonies and concerts for my birthday, at Christmas or whenever I did anything he considered especially worthwhile.

One day Larry said to me, 'When I retire, Joe, I want you to take over from me. You've really got it in you to make a foreman mat maker and trainer — we're all very impressed with your work and your potential.'

I think I disappointed him then and there when I replied, 'Mr Doyle, I don't want to be a mat maker. I want to be a musician and work with a band.'

'You can forget about that, Joe. There isn't a steady living in it. Just concentrate on this job and you'll never be out of work.'

He never gave up on me, but he was mistaken. I made music my career, while the mat factory was closed down two years after I left it.

* * *

The coconut fibre from which the mats were made came to us in enormous three-hundredweight bales from India. We would open these bales with a big hook, the dust getting everywhere, making us cough and hurting our eyes. We would then strip off the yarn in layers; these layers of yarn would be thick with dust also. Then we would have to unwind the yarn using a gadget called a spinner; again dust was everywhere, getting into our eyes, down our throats, inside our clothes. We then had to wind the unwound yarn into balls. There was a special way of doing this — if you got it wrong, the whole lot could ravel and it would take you a whole day trying to get it unravelled, and there would be holy war. Although I was his favourite, Larry was not above giving me a right rollicking if I stepped out of line or got the yarn in a tangle.

The coarse fibre was terribly hard on hands, and mine were often bleeding from handling it. I worried about my hands as I still hoped to be a pianist and it wasn't reassuring to think that in time they would get callused and lose their sensitivity.

There were five looms in the mat shop, all hand-operated, making a terrible clatter as you banged them down. Normally, trainees were not allowed on the looms until they had done six months' training, but I found myself working on them after only a month.

I was working late one evening — we had to get an order out quickly as it was overdue. Only Larry and I were left to finish the work. At last it was done and I was putting things away for the night. There was a big storeroom at the end of the shop in which were kept the finished mats, huge balls of yarn, the unopened bales, and various bits and pieces. I carried two large bales of yarn to the long cupboard under the high table. I pushed back the sliding doors and put both arms inside the cupboard to place the bales in position, when suddenly I felt two big rats scurrying up my arms. I screamed as they jumped over my shoulders onto the shop floor and scuttled towards the back door. Larry threw the huge pair of shears he'd been using to trim the ends of the finished mats and, whether by luck of judgment, he caught one of the horrid creatures, cutting it clean in half. Whether it was from fright, shock or the smell, I don't know, but I vomited right then and there.

'You'll have to clean that up,' Larry said.

I thought he meant the remains of the rat. 'I'm not touching that bloody thing,' I shouted.

'No, I'll look after that. You can clean up your own mess, and cut out that language.'

I was severely shaken, and I didn't go near that cupboard again for a long time. Following that episode, we got the vermin exterminators in, but really it was a waste of time — we always had the rats. They would nest in the yarn.

I had some further encounters with the disgusting creatures while working in Brunswick Road. I could always hear them scurrying around in the storeroom. It was a dark room and if I had to go in to collect something, naturally I didn't have to turn on a light, so I would surprise the rats and they would scurry over my feet as I went into the storeroom. Ugh! It was awful. To this day, I cringe when I think of them.

* * *

The second person who helped me tremendously in those days was my music teacher, Alan Mapson. I was allowed to take two hours off work for my music lessons every week. These took place in the building where we were doing our training, so I was also free to practise in the evenings. Alan had a music room upstairs, and to me it was a fabulous room, containing as it did a sweet-sounding piano. But best of all, there was a record player and a wonderful selection of records. Alan Mapson was an extremely quiet spoken man, gentle and very patient, especially with me.

My lessons would last an hour. Twenty minutes was 'practical' — actually learning to play pieces; twenty minutes was theory of music; and twenty minutes was musical appreciation. The latter would consist of listening to and discussing parts of a symphony, or big band records, or we might even listen to and discuss a pop record of the day. Alan's musical philosophy was that there were many musical roads down which we could travel and we should try them all, appreciating the good in all of them and throwing out the rubbish. 'Rubbish doesn't only apply to pop music,' he would say. 'Like what you like, not what other people tell you you ought to like.' Good sense and good advice.

On one occasion, after I had done especially well at an examination, Alan brought me to the Philharmonic Hall for a concert. The Liverpool Philharmonic Orchestra was playing Dvořák's *New World Symphony*. For a number of lessons before the concert, Alan gave me instruction on how a symphony is constructed and pointed out what I should listen for in the work. We went to the concert and it was wonderful. Afterwards, he brought me to meet the conductor, Malcolm Sargent (this was before they made him Sir).

I was also allowed to handle some of the instruments of the orchestra. Although I could recognise the sound of an oboe, I had no idea what an oboe looked like, or a bassoon, a French horn or the huge concert harp. The memory of that visit to the 'Phil' as we called it stays with me to this day, and Dvořák's *New World Symphony* is still my favourite classical piece.

When I had been studying with Alan Mapson for two years, he emigrated to Australia. He was someone I could look up to and respect, and since I had been obliged to end my education and train as a mat maker, my music lessons with Alan had become even more important to me. I relied on him.

I had thought for some time that there was something on his mind. One day he told me that, although he had always thought he was an orphan, he had discovered that he had a brother in Australia. Soon afterwards, he left without any goodbyes. I think he did this because he'd been in institutions ever since he was a child, and farewells would have made leaving even harder for him.

I knew he was going, but that didn't alter the fact that someone I trusted had simply disappeared from my life. To say I was shattered is an understatement. In fact, I was so upset that I gave up my music studies altogether. I felt that no one could teach me like Alan. This was a pity as I was only one exam away from obtaining my teaching diploma, and I was only eighteen at the time.

All through my life I have carried with me the memory of Alan Mapson. He shaped my whole musical thinking. For years I wondered how he was getting on in Australia, and finally, some years ago, I decided I would try to look for his address and endeavour to contact him. It took me a long time, lots of research, writing, phone calls and letters, but wonder of wonders, recently, through the West Australian Society for the Blind, I found him.

One day, not so long ago, I answered my telephone at about eleven o'clock in the morning. A voice said quietly, 'Is that Joe Bollard?'

'It is,' I answered.

'Do you know who this is?'

'I haven't an idea.'

'This is Alan Mapson calling from Australia.' You could have knocked me down with a feather, and there were tears in my eyes as we talked — his quiet, gentle voice coming all that way across the world. We now keep in contact. To my mind he is a musical genius and a wonderful teacher.

~ Seven ~

A few doors up from the Catholic Blind Asylum was a chemist's shop. Shortly after I started my training I had occasion to go there, and it was then that I first met Christine. She worked there as a shop assistant, and as soon as she spoke to me, I was smitten. Christine had a soft, gentle voice, a lovely warm disposition, and wore the most seductive-smelling perfume. Her laugh was like tinkling bells, or so I thought. She was a little older than I was, but to me that didn't matter. I was determined to get a date with this angel from heaven.

I would visit the chemist's shop every day on some pretext or other: my day wasn't complete unless I had heard Christine's voice speaking to me. I would buy something, probably something I didn't need, then I'd pretend to lose my way leaving the shop so that she'd come around from behind the counter, take my arm and lead me to the door. In my bedroom at home I had a huge hoard of elastoplasts, razor blades, headache tablets — all purchases made in order to have an excuse to visit Christine.

Obviously, there are aspects of sexuality which must always be absent from a blind person's life. We have nothing to gain by having girlie magazines hidden under the mattress or pictures of page-three girls pinned to the bathroom door.

Most men who can see are first attracted to a woman by visual factors — long blonde hair, a smiling face, white skin, a gorgeous figure. More than likely, all these things would attract me if I could see, but the fact that the visual side of sexuality is missing from my life, to my mind increases all the other factors. Sensuality is very important to me. I am an emotional man and need physical contact. I am easily aroused by sounds (particularly music) and by smells — certain perfumes send me bananas. A woman's voice and her speech can be a real turn on for me.

One of the reasons why a pleasant voice is so vital is that we lack that most important ingredient — eye contact. Sighted people can talk to one another with their eyes, sending messages of praise or disapproval across a room. A look can speak volumes. This is something that is missing for us.

For me to be attracted to a woman, she must have personality, a sense of humour, warmth, tenderness and understanding. I was sure that Christine had all these virtues in abundance.

* * *

The seeing person in a relationship with a blind one has to be very understanding, tolerant and patient. They must be able to show warmth and caring without being patronising or schmaltzy because of the other person's blindness. Of course, in the 1950s, being the blind man in a relationship meant that the traditional roles had to be reversed. For instance, when out for the evening, she would pick him up in the car, she would read the menu, she would read the bill at the end of the meal, and she would drive him home at the end of the evening. Nowadays there is nothing very unusual in this, but at that time, it was an added difficulty to be overcome by blind men.

I've had some strange experiences going out with women who could see. She wouldn't have a clue as to what to do or not to do or say. I would spend most of the evening trying to put her at her ease. After all, I'm just a normal human being whose eyes don't work.

On one such evening, I had made arrangements to meet a woman for a meal in a restaurant which was very popular and always crowded. I didn't bring my white cane to the restaurant, partly because I felt it might be off-putting to the lady, as this was before the days of the folding cane. Anyway, I hated carrying it and was secretly embarrassed by the bloody thing.

I took a taxi to the restaurant, and the taxi-driver brought me to the entrance where I was handed over to a waiter who brought me to our table. When the lady eventually arrived, I thought I'd be chivalrous and help her off with her coat. I wasn't aware that she was turning around towards me, and I reached out and put my clumsy hand straight onto her rather large breast.

'Oops! That's a good start, Bollard,' I told myself, as the woman laughed nervously. Then she handed me the menu. I handed it back to her.

'You read it,' I suggested.

Again that nervous laugh.

We decided we wouldn't have soup — we'd go straight for the main course. When it arrived, I adjusted my napkin on my lap, then started searching for my fork. Suddenly it arrived in my mouth with a lump of mashed potato on it. She actually thought she had to feed me! After a great deal of explanation, I managed to get it across to her that I was quite capable of feeding myself, which came as a great relief to her, I'm sure.

She spent the evening apologising for using the words 'look', 'see', 'watch', 'television', 'cinema', 'pictures', which she thought would 'hurt the feelings of a blind person'. I tried to explain to her that we use these words ourselves. I told her that blind people do go to the cinema and we do enjoy television. We may need a little help at times regarding description of a scene, but generally we cope, using a little common sense.

After the meal, we decided we'd go for a walk in the park as it was a fine summer's night, but first I expressed a wish to visit the Gents. I certainly wasn't prepared for what happened next. The lady asked to see the manager, and when he arrived she quietly asked him if the gents' toilet could be emptied of men so that she could take her blind friend into the toilet and show him where things were! 'You've got a kinky one here, Bollard,' I told myself.

Nothing of the sort. Again, she just didn't know what to do. I asked the manager if he could take me to the door of the Gents and leave me there, I'd find my own way after that.

On entering the loo, I felt my way along the wall until I came to where I thought the urinals were situated. I found the step that is usually in front of the urinals and was about to point Percy at the porcelain when a voice in front of me yelled,

'Hey you, you're pissing in my back pocket!'

There was somebody already occupying the urinal. I stepped back and fell off the step with Percy still prominent, picked myself up and groped my way to the next one. As I relieved myself, the voice beside me said to his friend, 'Hey Tommy, this fellow's half pissed.'

I thought he should have applied the remark to himself when you consider that he almost got half what I wanted to get rid of over his backside!

* * *

As for my one-sided romance with Christine, it came to an abrupt end about six weeks after it started. One day I called at the shop during my lunch hour for my daily dose of 'turn on', only to find the shop closed. A passer-by informed me that there was a notice in the window stating:

CLOSED UNTIL FURTHER NOTICE

The chemist's shop reopened six weeks later under new management. I learned that Christine, light of my life, the subject of all my fantasies, the centre of my dreams, had run away with the proprietor of the shop. He had left his wife and five children and eloped to Australia with my pharmaceutical nymphet.

Such is teenage life.

~ Eight ~

By the time I left the mat shop at Brunswick Road, at the age of nineteen, my life had completely changed.

Alan Mapson's departure had upset me so much that I'd given up studying music and I hadn't played at all for about ten months. Then, at a friend's wedding, I heard a woman attempting to play the piano and I thought that even if I couldn't play better than that, I knew I couldn't be any worse, so I had a go.

My musical education was classical and I didn't know any songs except 'Daisy Daisy' and 'I'll be Your Sweetheart', so I played these over and over while the wedding guests waltzed and sang along. Something told me they wouldn't appreciate a recital of Bach and Mozart!

It gave me a great buzz to be playing again and to know that my efforts were appreciated. I made up my mind there and then that I wanted to be a musician and work professionally as a piano player.

Soon I was getting bits and pieces of work playing here and there at various parties and functions. I also played the accordion and was in demand, especially at weekends. At this time I still had some time to go training as a mat-maker.

* * *

One place where I used to play at weekends was the Merseyside Social Club for the Blind in Huskison Street. This club was run by blind people for blind people. We used to play a version of bingo there, and even darts — dangerous but fun! Somebody would tap the dart board so that you would know where it was, then they'd run away quickly and you would throw the dart. I was useless at this — I often got double wall or double floor.

We had a good music scene there, as being blind, there were plenty of musicians. We got a four-piece band going, and I was the dogsbody, playing accordion one night, piano the next and singing. The place had its own bar, also run by partially sighted people, and a good deal of drinking went on.

One Saturday night I was playing at the club when I was approached by a man who said he liked my piano playing and asked would I like a job playing at a nightclub. Needless to say, I jumped at the chance. I arranged to meet the man again on the following Friday night, and he brought me to a dingy little hovel somewhere in Liverpool 8. This was a part of Liverpool where many poor Black and Asian immigrants lived, and it had a reputation for being dangerous, but that didn't bother me. It turned out that the man who had offered me the job was the drummer in the club, and he introduced me to the bass player. We were to be the trio for the night.

When we started to play, the place was empty — or so I thought, but apparently there was one couple on the floor. A man with a pseudo-American accent sauntered up to the little bandstand and asked could we play 'I Can't Give You Anything But Love, Baby'. He was with a big blonde and was lurching with her around the tiny dance floor. When we'd finished playing, he came and asked if we wanted a drink. The drummer and bass player both said they'd have a whiskey, so I, wanting to sound experienced, asked for a Scotch on the rocks. I had no idea what it was, and, when it came, I stupidly drank it down in great gulps, trying to show off. I didn't like the taste, but I wasn't going to tell the others that, and later, when more customers wanted to buy us drinks, I had the same again.

We played well into the early hours of the following morning. By the time we were finished, I was absolutely legless. I got five guineas for my night's work and ordered a taxi to take me home, but when the driver saw the state I was in, he refused to take me. At last, I managed to persuade another driver to take me back to Everton. I crawled into the house at about four o'clock in the morning and my mother heard me coming in. She asked whether I was all right and didn't guess that I was drunk. I told her I'd been at a friend's house and wasn't feeling very well. I crept into bed, feeling dreadful, but I had five guineas in my jacket pocket and I felt that at last I was beginning to make it as a musician.

The following Friday I again played in the nightclub and got even more drunk. There was a terrible row the next morning at home as my mother now realised I had come home drunk. She had given up drinking herself, and I think she was worried that I was going the same way as my parents. She asked where I'd been, and I told her I had a job in a club down in the 'South End' as it was called.

'And I suppose it's full of prostitutes,' she remarked.

I had no idea what a prostitute was, and again wanting to sound like a man of the world, I put my big foot in it. 'Yes it is and I get plenty of tips from them and they like my piano playing,' I replied.

'I hope you don't go with any of those women,' she said, horrified.

'What women? I'm not interested in women. I'm too busy playing the piano.' I still had no idea about the real world and what went on in it.

I went to the same club the next Friday and halfway through the night I was so drunk that I fell off the piano stool. That was the final straw for the manager who ordered me a taxi and told me not to come back again. 'You can't handle your drink, lad,' he told me.

I was shattered. I had blown my chance of getting into the 'big time' as I called it.

* * *

Meanwhile, I was in trouble at Brunswick Road with Larry Doyle, for arriving at work late and hungover. He had already told me that I would have to choose between mats and music, and I had, of course, opted for music.

I finally left the Catholic Blind Institute when I was nineteen. I had finished my training and had qualified as a fully fledged mat-maker. It was expected that I would go on to work in the 'Sheltered Workshop' in Cornwallis Street. This time I refused point blank. I was determined to be a professional musician — it didn't matter where, as long as I could get work playing the piano.

For the next few months, I worked in various clubs in the South End of Liverpool, most of them dingy little places down in cellars, and although I was drinking fairly heavily, I managed to hide it from my family. I would get home in the early hours of the morning when they were in bed, and crawl up the stairs, as drunk as a skunk. I didn't keep jobs long, as the managers of the clubs wouldn't put up with my drinking and would tell me not to come back the following week. My playing was all done at weekends, usually Friday and Saturday nights.

The club work diminished, and I found myself playing at private functions: birthday parties, engagement parties and sometimes a do at Christmas or on New Year's Eve. These didn't pay very well, but I was also getting National Assistance which was a sort of dole. This enabled me to give my mother something towards my keep, although it wasn't a lot.

* * *

It was at a private party that the most horrible experience of my life occurred. I have never spoken about it, and even now the memory of it disturbs me. It's an example of how a person with a disability can be dreadfully used and abused. It also highlights how wrong and unforgivable was the total lack of instruction, information and preparation for life after boarding school.

One evening, shortly before my nineteenth birthday, a blind friend of mine asked me to play at a do in his house. We agreed on a price for the job and he told me to be there after pub-closing time, which in those days was at half past ten.

I took a taxi to the house and began to play after they had all come back from the pub. It was quite a large house on the outskirts of Liverpool, and people milled around, chatting, eating and drinking. My instructions were to play until one o'clock in the morning and, for once, I didn't drink much — just a glass of wine when I arrived. I was too much taken with the fabulous piano, and I was really enjoying playing it.

Not long after I began, two men came and stood beside the

piano, and began to talk to me about my playing. They seemed really interested and I thought that they might be club owners who would be able to put some work in my way. I really turned it on and played everything they asked me. They tried to get me to drink, but I wanted to keep my head clear so that I could play better and impress them, so I refused.

People began to drift away as the evening came to a close, and the man who'd booked me said that he was going somewhere else, and I could ring for a taxi when I'd finished — the phone was at the foot of the stairs, somebody would show me where.

At one o'clock, I got up from the piano and was immediately approached by the two men who'd been talking to me earlier. 'I want to ring for a taxi,' I said.

'Someone's using the phone at the foot of the stairs, but there's another upstairs. We'll show you where.' One man went upstairs in front of me, while the other followed behind.

'There's a phone in here,' one of them said, as he led me into the room on the right.

As soon as we were inside, the man behind me kicked the door shut. The man in front turned around, grabbed my arms, twisting them up my back and dragged me towards the bed, while the other kicked me in the back, sending me sprawling face downwards on the bed and jumped on top of me. I struggled, but the other man knelt on my neck and held a pillow down over my head. I was terrified that I'd smother. Meanwhile, the man behind me pulled down my pants and underpants and dropped his own pants. I was frantic — and half-suffocated — but they were laughing hysterically and muttering obscenities.

Then the man on top of me drove his penis right into my back passage; the pain was excruciating. I tried to scream but the pillow muffled the noise, while the man on top of me fondled my genitals, gurgling with delight. The man holding me down encouraged him, getting more and more excited. When the first man had finished, the second tried to have his turn, but he couldn't make it. He got on top of me while the first guy knelt on my neck, but he must have come before he could enter me.

As suddenly as it had begun, it was over. One of the men kicked me in the ribs and they both turned and ran downstairs. They must have been pulling up their pants as they went, because they ran straight out the front door and I heard no more.

I must have fainted, as it was some time later that I managed to lift myself off the bed. I remembered where the toilet was, made my way there and, having got violently sick, cleaned myself up as best I could. I used toilet paper as padding, because some of the discharge was probably blood, and I knew I would have to take a taxi home. Before I went downstairs, I found a door next to the door of the room I'd been in, and I could hear people beyond it. Judging by the noises I heard, they weren't the slightest bit interested in visitors, so I made my way down to the phone and ordered a taxi. It seemed an age before it arrived, and while I was waiting I had to go to the toilet to get sick again.

Luckily, when I got home at last, everyone was in bed. I cleaned myself up again, fell into bed and began to tremble. I shook and shook. I wept, trying not to make a noise in case someone heard me. I was in a severe state of shock, and in pain. Eventually I fell asleep and had horrible nightmares. I didn't get up the next day. My mother sent up food, thinking that I'd been on a drinking spree and was suffering the consequences. I couldn't tell anyone. I felt terrible, dirty and ashamed, and I couldn't stop trembling.

The next day, I went to my doctor, an extremely gentle, quiet-spoken character, who thought the world of me. Having examined me and listened to my story, he wanted to phone the police. Homosexuality was against the law in those days, and rape has always been a crime. However, I didn't want any publicity, and he reluctantly agreed not to call the police. No permanent physical harm had been done, but I was in a bad state of shock, and he gave me some tablets to steady my nerves, and some sleeping pills.

That evening, I phoned the man in whose house all this had taken place. He, of course, refused to believe me. Then he said that he didn't know half the people who'd been at the party, and even hinted that I'd lcd thc two guys on. If I called the police, he said, he would deny all knowledge of anything that went on — and how could I have been so stupid as to let two men bring me into a bedroom? Asking for trouble, he said.

Trouble? It wouldn't have occurred to me. I was extremely thin and not at all robust, weighing about seven and a half stone. I had had no experience of violence apart from a few fights at school. I'd heard of women being raped, but never men. I knew there were 'queers', as they were then called ('gay' meant something different then), I even knew a couple. What I didn't know was what they actually *did*. I certainly wasn't homosexual, and anyway I was more interested in drink than in sex at that time.

My family never knew what had happened. They knew I was ill, but I told them it was a combination of flu and a bad hangover after a big drinking session.

* * *

There were other things too that I was learning about life — things that I should have been learning when I was thirteen.

I was so naïve that I didn't learn about girls having periods and using sanitary towels until I was seventeen. One evening at home, I trapped my fingers in the toilet door. They bled profusely, so I rushed into my sisters' bedroom, which was the nearest, to find something to wrap around my hand. Two of my sisters were at home at the time. On the dressing table, I found just the thing — a package of what felt like bandages. They even had a loop at each end so I could tie the bandage properly. I had this bandage on my hand until supper time when my mother yelled, 'What's that you've got on your hand?'

I tried to explain, but there seemed to be consternation. My mother ripped my bandage off and scolded me severely for going into the girls' room. My younger sister started to cry, while Sue, who is two years older than I am, whispered, 'I'll tell you later.'

That evening, she explained to me about girls having periods and using sanitary towels, which they could buy in the chemist's shop. I was astounded. Being in a boarding school run by nuns may have been brilliant academic training, but as regards preparing me for life in the real world, it was a dismal failure.

~ *Nine* ~

One passion which I have in my life to this day is my love of sport. I am a fanatical soccer enthusiast, particularly where Everton Football Club is concerned, and although I don't get there as often as I'd like, I try to go a couple of times a season.

It all began when I was twelve years old. One Saturday, my brother Bill, Maurice Finnegan who lived next door and I were playing in Stanley Park, a huge park separating Everton and Liverpool Football Grounds. Suddenly I heard this great roar. 'What's that?' I asked.

'It's the crowd at Goodison Park,' Maurice replied. 'Everton are playing at home today.'

'Let's go and have a look,' I suggested.

'It costs money to get in there,' Bill warned us.

'Come on and see if we can get in for nothing,' I pleaded. 'It sounds great.' We made our way to the big gate at Goodison Park and a man told us that if we waited ten minutes he'd let us in free as there wasn't much time left in the game. Everton were playing Charlton Athletic. I'd heard these names on the wireless but never thought I could actually get to a match.

The excitement I felt when we were finally let in simply can't be put into words. I still get that thrill from a football game. There seemed to be something alive in the buzz of the crowd. I had butterflies in my stomach. Maurice and Bill told me what was happening, and I could tell a lot from the sound the crowd made. If you're watching a match and shut your eyes and listen to the crowd instead of the commentary, you get a good idea of how things are going — the crowd's always there seconds ahead of the commentator anyway, no matter how good he is. It might take you a few minutes to identify the sides but then you get to know from the oohs and aahs where the ball is and if the player has missed it.

From that day, I have been an Everton fanatic. The game was a one-one draw and I can remember it clearly — or the little time I was there — even though it is fifty years ago. I couldn't stop talking about it and was well and truly smitten.

In 1948 my sister Margaret married her boyfriend, Pat Anderson, an ardent Evertonian who encouraged my love for Everton Football Club. One day he offered to take me to a game. It was a big game and as we walked to Goodison Park, Pat gave me a run-down on the history of the club, telling me about Dixie Deane and other former great Everton players. When we got to the ground, Pat read his programme to me and during the match he gave me a great commentary. It was fabulous and, as we walked home, we carried out a post mortem on the game. I was in seventh heaven.

Pat continued to take me to Everton home games for the next nine years or so, and we also went to many away games. We went to Burnley, Bolton, Bury, Manchester, Derby, Aston Villa, Lincoln City, Sheffield, Leeds, Oldham — all great adventures and wonderful memories. In the days when I had little money, Pat treated me to my train fare and match ticket, as well as many a meat pie and cup of tea. I still remember many of the games we went to together during the 1950s. We even went to the reserve games when we couldn't get away to the senior matches. I can rhyme off the team of that era. When I left Liverpool, what I missed most — after my family, of course — were my visits to Goodison Park.

When I was at Brunswick Road, making mats, I wrote to Clive Britton, then manager of Everton, inviting him to a concert I'd helped to put together. To my amazement, he accepted and, not only did he come himself, but he brought along the Everton captain Peter Farrell, Tommy Eglington and goalkeeper Jimmy O'Neill. Peter and I remained friends, and when I returned to Ireland he constantly met me at matches and we swapped stories of former Everton days.

I remember crying unashamedly when Everton beat Sheffield Wednesday in the 1966 FA Cup. In 1953, Everton reached the semi-final where they played Bolton Wanderers and were expected to beat them easily. The game was played at Maine Road, Manchester, and Everton were three-nil down after twelve minutes, and four down at half-time. Clive Britton, the Everton manager, had promised me that if Everton got to Wembley I could travel to the final with the players. In the second half, Everton came back, scoring three goals, and with two minutes to go it was four-three, but we just couldn't make it. We lost, and I thought it was the saddest day of my life.

Even now, the thrill of going to a soccer match stays with me. The atmosphere is great, and of course I have someone with me to fill in. Whether it's my own local team, Bray Wanderers, at the Carlisle grounds, or an international at Landsdowne Road, I sit in the stand and shout and yell for my team with everybody else, while I listen to the commentary.

* * *

I also have a great interest in horse racing, especially steeplechasing. I backed my first horse when I was twelve years old. It was called Right Monkey and won at 100 to 6. I had a shilling each way on it and thought I was a millionaire. Living not too far from Aintree, I went twice to the Grand National with my brother Paddy. What a thrill. We saw Sundew win in 1957 and Mr What in 1958.

I love the sport and, if I could have a wish come true, it would be to ride in the Grand National. I keep recordings of past races, both audio and video, and I love to play them over and over. I used to dream about riding Arkle — what a horse!

* * *

Shortly after my twentieth birthday, I started to go out regularly with a girl from the South End of Liverpool. Vera was her name. I can't remember how we first met, but we used to go to the pictures or the theatre. Sometimes we'd go to Southport, about twenty miles north of Liverpool, for a day out.

I was still drinking heavily, and how Vera put up with me for as long as she did, I'll never know. We had one special arrangement. On Thursday nights she would stay at home and wash her hair, and I would stay at home and listen to records or the radio. We got engaged on my twenty-first birthday, and I got pissed as usual. Vera brought me home in a taxi, and we had a row about my drinking. When I think now of having a row on the day we got engaged — I was a disgrace.

We planned to get married the following April and I actually tried to start saving. We spent a good Christmas at parties in friends' houses. I wasn't getting much work now: my reputation as a drinker and messer had got around the various clubs and no one wanted to know me.

On St Patrick's Day 1957, I'd made plans to meet Vera in the afternoon, go to the pictures and then for a meal. She rang about noon.

'Hello, Joe, it's me, Vera —' I thought she was going to cancel our date and tried to interrupt, but she went on. 'Listen, Joe, I'm breaking off our engagement. I've met someone else, I've been meeting him every Thursday night when you thought I was washing my hair. I'm very sorry. I'll send your ring back during the week. Thanks for everything.'

I couldn't believe it. The room seemed to be spinning. Luckily I was alone at home. I dropped into a chair and sat with my head in my hands, fighting tears. We were only four weeks away from our wedding. I'd arranged everything for it and now it was off, our engagement broken on the telephone.

My mother was glad it was ended, as she didn't approve of Vera. But I did love her — we didn't have sex, but she was fun to be with when I was sober. For weeks I wandered around in a daze, hating all women.

* * *

After the breaking off of our engagement, I began to think more and more about an idea I'd had before meeting Vera — going back to Ireland to work. I'd put it out of my mind, as Vera didn't want to go, but now it seemed a great idea. When I suggested it to my mother, she was totally against it.

'Who's going to look after you?' she said. 'There's nobody in Ireland who could take care of you, and your Uncle Dickie's at work all day — he wouldn't be able to mind you.' But being taken care of by my uncle wasn't what I had in mind.

One day, one of my sisters read an advertisement in the *Melodymaker* newspaper: a band in the west of Ireland was looking for a piano player. I wrote, saying that I was a blind pianist, familiar with most of the musical arrangements being used by bands at the time. I waited and waited for a reply, drinking more and more. I was at a very low ebb when a telegram arrived with a message:

RING BALLINA CONCERNING JOB.

I asked my father where Ballina was.

'Jesus,' he said, 'you're not going to work with the culchies, are you?'

I rang the number and found that the man in question was Jack Ruane, who had a dance-band playing one-night stands all over Ireland. He told me to come over immediately for an audition. I told him I had no money for my ticket and he wired me some the following day.

After fourteen years in England, I had finally made the big decision to go back to Ireland.

~ Ten ~

When I left home to return to Ireland, I had reached an all-time low in my life. I was drinking like a fish and had few friends left besides drinking pals. I had become slovenly, a know-all, a cheeky smart-arse who could play the piano, but whom nobody would employ because he was a messer.

I was playing in 'dives' for want of better employment, never happier than when I was sitting at a piano, half-pissed, with a row of full glasses across the top of it. Well, I thought I was happy.

My mother had been a heavy drinker herself until my brother Richard's death in Palestine in 1948, when serving with the British Army. She didn't give up drinking entirely, but she certainly cut down on it, and she 'got religion'. She made pilgrimages to Lourdes and Walsingham; she joined the Women's Sodality in the local parish; and, not having been a regular Mass-goer, she began going to church on Sundays, and sometimes during the week.

My father didn't take to this at all. Tension built up, and there were many rows and some dreadful scenes. Shortly after I left, they separated. My father went to live with my sister Margaret, and over the next few years lived with various members of the family.

My parents were reconciled and reunited shortly before my father's death. He wrote a beautiful letter to me, apologising for any hurt he might have caused me, saying he would love to come to visit me in Ireland. His letter went on:

> ... perhaps we could go fishing again at Greystones, Joe (remember the good old days?) I know I might not have been the greatest father in the world, I'm just a Dublin Jackeen

> cum soldier cum navvy cum dock labourer. I was always very proud of you Joe, and the way you succeeded in overcoming your blindness....

My father never did come back to Ireland; he died in 1972, aged seventy, without fulfilling his dream. My mother died at the age of ninety-four.

* * *

31 July1957 was one of the most momentous days of my life. That day, I left Liverpool for the west of Ireland. Here I was, at twenty-one years of age, on the threshold of a new life. I should have been excited, but as I sat on the deck of the Dublin boat that night, I felt desperately lost and alone. Most musicians would have been thrilled at the prospect of joining Jack Ruane's band — but I just felt wretched.

I was broke as usual and couldn't afford a cabin, so I sat on deck all night. Luckily it was a fine summer night. It was the height of the tourist season, so the boat was packed with holiday-makers and I couldn't sleep. I sat, feeling thoroughly sorry for myself, thinking how I would miss my family and friends, my Saturday afternoons at Goodison Park, Saturday night visits to the club, long walks on Sundays, the sounds and smells of my city of Liverpool.

I wanted to be left alone with my thoughts, but sitting beside me was a talkative lady who told me her life story. She was from Birkenhead and was travelling to Dublin to visit her late husband's people.

I was hungover after a farewell party and perhaps she took my silence for keen interest, but I was actually asking myself would she never stop. At last, around three in the morning, she put her arms around me, laid her head on my shoulder and fell fast asleep.

When I left Liverpool, my total worldly possessions consisted of a shabby little suitcase containing two pairs of socks, two pairs of threadbare underpants, one clean but well-worn shirt, an old toothbrush, a razor with a half-empty packet of blades, and a bow tie. The last was something that no musician would be without in those days: having a bow tie could mean the difference between getting and not getting a gig. On leaving Liverpool, my friends had given me a bottle of wine, which I began to drink as soon as the woman fell asleep. I had some cigarettes in my pocket and a very small amount of money.

As the night wore on, people fell asleep and it became quieter. I could feel the vibrations from the ship's engines as we chugged through the summer night, and I sat there with my white cane beside me and began to wonder what I'd let myself in for.

Suddenly I began to feel this dreadful panic building up inside me. What had I done? I'd shut the door on a life which, although perhaps not the happiest in the world, at least had some sort of security, and now I was on my own. I was setting out on an adventure, broke, baffled and blind. Huddled on the bench, I began to tremble with sheer fright.

The woman sleeping on my shoulder stirred. 'Are you cold, son?' she asked, cuddling closer.

'No.' My voice sounded choked as I answered.

She went to sleep again, tightening her arms around me. I finished the wine and the misery grew. Around half past five, my sleeping partner stirred, stretched, kissed me and stood up. 'Would you like something to eat?' she asked.

'If you could just get me a cup of tea,' I replied.

She went away and returned twenty minutes later with tea and a couple of sandwiches. 'Where are you heading for when we get off the boat?' she asked.

'Westland Row Station.'

'So am I — we can travel together, there's a bus that meets this boat, so they told me downstairs.'

Thank God for ships that pass in the night, I thought to myself.

We arrived at Westland Row around ten to eight in the morning, and all the time my companion, whose name was Margaret, kept up a running commentary. Normally I'm one of those blind people who like to be told what's going on around them, but I was feeling worse than ever and didn't want to listen. The poor woman even paid for my bus fare.

I'd bought my ticket to Ballina before I left Liverpool, so I didn't have to go to the ticket office in the station. Margaret placed me in the hands of a station official, and before leaving me she kissed me fervently, gave me a warm hug and wished me well in my new career.

'I'll look out for your name in the papers,' she laughed, 'and some day when you're famous I can say, "I met him once."'

I thanked her sincerely. As she walked away, she called back to me, 'Good luck, Joe, maybe we'll meet again sometime.'

We did meet again, but not until much water had flowed under the bridge.

* * *

The journey to Ballina was horrendous. I was under the impression that Ballina was only a short run from Dublin and when the ticket collector came round about an hour into the journey I asked him what time we were due to arrive.

'Ten minutes to three,' he said. 'Change at Manulla.' It was then about ten past nine in the morning.

'But that's hours away,' I moaned.

'It's a long trip from Dublin to Ballina,' he informed me. 'That's the trouble with you English, you think Ireland is a tiny little island.' At that time I had a strong Liverpool accent, but even today I get annoyed when people call me 'English'.

'I'm Irish, but my geography isn't very good,' I retorted.

The journey went on and on. Naturally I couldn't read the names of the stations and they didn't call them out as we approached, as they do on main lines today. I could have been going through Timbuktu for all I knew. I worried that I would miss the connection at Manulla Junction and get carried on to Westport. I had to ask someone where we were. Around lunch-time, I began to feel physically sick. I'd been partying for two days before I left Liverpool, I hadn't slept on the boat, I'd hardly eaten anything and had drunk a bottle of wine.

Eventually we arrived in Ballina. I picked up my case and my white cane and stepped down onto the platform. Then I just stood and waited, not knowing where to go. I heard someone walking towards me and was about to speak when a voice said, 'Who are you?'

'I could ask you the same question,' I replied.

'I'm Jack Ruane.'

'And I'm Joe Bollard.'

'Jesus, son, you won't do!'

I can still remember standing on that platform — the smell of diesel, the sound of the train — and wondering what lay ahead. I recall the shock of Jack's words. I thought I'd soon be back on a train, going home. How could I explain that I'd made a mess of it? What could I tell my family? I'd burned my boats and simply couldn't face turning back. It wasn't as if I'd got the job — even if Jack didn't put me on the next train, I still had an audition to do.

I was at the lowest ebb in my life and I felt real despair. I was in a desperate state, mentally and physically. I said nothing, just allowed Jack to take me by the arm and lead me away.

He brought me to the van, saying as we walked, 'I'll get you a meal, you can have a good sleep and we'll put you on the train back to Dublin in the morning. You certainly couldn't stand up to life on the road as a band musician — you wouldn't last a week.'

I could hardly take in what he was saying and I didn't argue but went with him. Fair enough, I must have looked a right mess: I hadn't slept for three days, I needed a shave, my clothes were dishevelled from travelling, I was sick, cold, unbelievably tired. I was as skinny as a rake too, weighing about six stone ten. No wonder he wasn't impressed.

We drove to the digs he'd arranged for me. The landlady greeted me warmly and sat me down at the table for a meal, but I was so sick and shattered that I couldn't eat anything. She showed me my room and, as I undressed, I could hear the people downstairs talking about me.

Jack's voice was raised: 'He won't do at all — did you see him? He looks terrible.'

Another male voice replied, 'Well, he's travelled a long way, Jack.'

'Maybe, but he'll have to go back to Liverpool tomorrow.'

'You can't send him back without hearing him play. He might be just what you're looking for. He might be another George Shearing.' (Some chance, I thought.)

'Okay,' Jack replied. 'I'll tell you what we'll do. We're going away on a week's tour starting tomorrow. You keep him here at my expense and feed him up, let him sit out in the sun and get some colour into his cheeks, and when we get back we'll give him an audition.'

I crawled into bed and lay there listening to the birds singing — it was still only afternoon. The sun was shining, but all I wanted was to sleep. A great wave of loneliness enveloped me. I felt so alone in this strange country, with people who didn't want me. I was broke, exhausted, jobless ... perhaps about to be sent back in a week's time, which would be even worse than staying. I began to cry, tears running down my cheeks. Oh God, what was I going to do?

Finally, I fell into a deep sleep.

~ Eleven ~

I didn't wake up until noon the following day, and I felt totally confused. Strange sounds came to my ears — a donkey was braying pitifully close by, there seemed to be millions of jackdaws just outside my window. Gone was the heavy rumble of traffic, the hoot of a ship from the docks, the whine of a factory siren, the whistle of a far-off train, the sound of a tram clanking down Aubrey Street. City sounds. For the next seven years I would wake to the screeching of crows and jackdaws, lowing cattle, braying donkeys and the ringing of church bells.

Sound is so important to blind people — we need it to paint a picture of our surroundings, in place of a visual image. Listening to sounds establishes where they are and what is going on around us. Sound sense, I call it.

I got up, washed, shaved, dressed and made my way tentatively down to the living room where Mrs Flynn, the landlady, came rushing to meet me. She grabbed be by the shoulder and shunted me to a chair. 'Did you sleep well, Joe?' she asked.

'Yes, thank you.'

'Would you like something to eat?'

I could smell the lunch cooking. 'Yes please, Mrs Flynn. I'm really hungry.'

'You'd like a cup of tea first, wouldn't you? And you must call me Marie, everyone does. I'll get you some tea and then I'll show you around the house.'

She sounded like a youngish woman, and I later found out that she was in her mid-thirties. Her accent seemed strange to my ears: it was the west of Ireland accent, and it took me some time to get used to this accent with many dialects, varying from the soft gentle sounds of Mayo through the hard, guttural accent of Roscommon and the fast-flowing speech of Galway.

As I drank my tea, Marie Flynn told me that she came from 'out the country' — Behybeg — but since her marriage to Jim Flynn who worked in Ballina Post Office, she had moved into town and taken in boarders. She had no family. 'God has decided not to send us any children,' she said sadly.

'Make allowances for me, Joe,' she continued. 'You are the first blind person I ever met and you must tell me what to do and what not to do. You're sharing a room with Frank Malone who plays the saxophone in Jack's band. He's from Belfast and he's a quiet lad — you'll like him. Jack's gone on a week's tour with the band to the North and we have to look after you and see you get plenty of rest and fresh air. His daughter will come every day and take you up to his house to practise the piano.'

After lunch, I sat out in the hot summer sun. The air was fresh, with a tinge of something — a smell I didn't recognise. I later discovered that it was the smell of turf, which was everywhere. Every household in Ballina seemed to burn it, and with my keen sense of smell I could get it all the time. In the pub sitting next to someone at the bar, you could smell turf from him. Kneeling at Mass, I could tell there was somebody beside me from the smell of turf. It got into people's clothes and hair; even in the shops I could smell it. It has occurred to me that the West of Ireland Tourist Board should bottle the smell and sell it to the Yanks, calling it '*Eau de Turf*'.

That evening, Anne Ruane called to the house and walked with me to Morrison Terrace where Jack lived. I played the piano for about an hour, then Anne walked back to the digs with me. She was about twelve and very quiet. I'm sure she was terrified of leading a blind man along, so I tried to put her at her ease by asking questions about Ballina. She told me about the River Moy, the Cathedral and the Town Hall where her father often played. In fact, the band was playing there the following week. 'That's where you'll probably start,' she said, but I wondered.

Marie Flynn's husband Jim came in late that evening, and I recognised the voice I'd heard the day before, persuading Jack not to send me back to Liverpool without hearing me play. Jim had a brusque manner. He was a hard man and I felt it wouldn't take much to rouse his temper. It was also obvious to me that he'd been drinking. He welcomed me to the house and took me on a tour, talking me through the various rooms. He made me count the stairs, showed me where everything was in the bathroom, where their room was, and made me do a 'dummy run' around the house so that I'd have the geography of it in my head.

This really surprised and pleased me. Here was this culchie, as my father would have called him, doing exactly the right thing for a blind person moving into a new environment, and I didn't have to ask. It was great.

For the rest of the week, I got up at lunch-time, ate a big meal and sat in the sun until Anne came to take me for my practice. We'd walk back, and I'd learn more and more about Ballina. I'd go to bed around eleven o'clock — but something was missing. I wanted a drink and I was beginning to feel it. I couldn't go to the pub as I didn't know the way, and anyway I had no money. Then, on Saturday night, Jim asked if I'd like to go for a drink. I jumped at the offer. On the way, I explained that I had no money, but Jim laughed it off. 'Don't worry, Joe. When you start work, you can bring me for a drink.'

I tried to keep my drinking down that night, not wanting to overdo it on my first week in the digs.

The following day, Jim came to Mass with me. It was a quarter past twelve Mass and it was packed, mostly with men. They all stood at the back of the church — nobody seemed to want to go up to the front. During Mass, there was a general hubbub from the men at the back, just inside the door. I tried to concentrate on the Mass, but couldn't help listening to various conversations, which were in full flow as the priest mumbled away in Latin. I couldn't believe my ears when I heard three lads actually playing cards while the Mass was in progress (they were playing pontoon), and there was that famous smell of turf. During the sermon, I was astounded to hear two men haggling over the price of a sheep that one was trying to sell to the other. On the way home, I asked Jim why these people bothered coming to Mass. 'Oh, they have to go to Mass. It's a mortal sin if they don't.'

* * *

On Tuesday afternoon, Jack Ruane called at the digs to take me to his house for the audition with the band. They were all packed into the long, narrow front room with the piano at the far end. It wasn't a great piano, but I'd played worse. All the musicians read music, except the bass player. 'We'll start with "Maryland, My Maryland",' Jack said.

I was delighted. It's an old Dixieland number and I knew it well. We then played 'In the Mood' — no problem there — then 'American Patrol' — all right so far. Jack made no comment, just announced the numbers. We played six or seven more numbers, including some jazz, which gave me the chance to take a couple of solos. I didn't do anything extraordinary but apparently everyone was impressed with my playing.

I did notice one strange thing about the band. The bass player came to the piano to ask for a 'G' to tune the double bass. Then, when he had it tuned, he started to play with the rest of us, but not in the same key. He was just plucking any old notes as long as there was a sound coming from the instrument. He had the right rhythm but no ear. We played one number in B flat and he played all the way through in F sharp. It was the weirdest sound I'd ever heard.

At the end of the audition, I stood up and all the musicians in the band applauded. Each one came and shook my hand and Jack introduced them individually. Then I got a surprise.

'This is my daughter, Phyllis,' Jack said. 'She plays alto sax with the band.' A woman musician? I hadn't met many of those.

After they'd gone, Jack and I sat down to discuss my position. I'd passed the audition with flying colours. 'You're a fine musician, son,' he said. 'I think you could do well. We must talk about money.'

He made me an offer and I was astounded. 'I couldn't live on that, Jack. After I'd paid my digs, there'd be hardly anything left for myself,' I said. 'I didn't come to Ballina for a holiday. I want to work with a band, but I have to make a living.'

Jack said nothing.

'I'm sorry, but if you aren't prepared to increase the amount, I'll have to go back to Liverpool.' I was adamant.

'All right, son, but don't tell the others what you're getting. It's very hard to make a living in the band business today — there's a lot of competition and a lot of overheads.'

We agreed on a weekly wage, which I insisted was for four nights only. If we played more, I'd get extra. Reluctantly he agreed and we shook hands. I had been rehearsing in Jack's house all week and hadn't met his wife, Maura. A shy person, she seldom entered the front room where the piano was kept. Now, however, he brought me into the kitchen, and Maura made tea for us. She was a nice, homely lady who didn't seem embarrassed by my blindness, but welcomed me to Ballina and made me feel at home.

While we sat drinking tea, Jack told me more about the make-up of the band. Jack himself played alto sax and clarinet, Phyllis played second alto, Frank Malone played lead tenor sax, Ciaran played second tenor. We had first and second trumpets — Denis and Aidan, no trombone although one joined us some time later, Tommy Murphy on drums and Billy Quigley on double bass. Johnny Bruen was the vocalist.

'Jack, I noticed something rather odd about the bass player,' I remarked. 'He wasn't playing in any of the keys we played in — he was just plonking any old notes.'

Jack explained that Billy wasn't a bass player; in fact, he wasn't a musician at all. An extra driver was needed on long journeys in the band wagon, and that was his job. The band also needed a bass player, but Jack couldn't afford both and the driver was more important. 'Anyway,' he argued, 'the punters don't know if the bass player's playing in the same key as the rest of the band.'

'The punters mightn't know, but any musician worth his salt would realise,' I pointed out.

'Don't worry about it, son, you'll get used to it.' I never did. Billy was a great wagon driver, though, and a hell of a nice guy.

My first gig was to be the following night, in the Town Hall in Ballina, playing at the Teachers' Dance. 'I'll introduce you to the crowd,' said Jack. 'And afterwards we'll do a little publicity with you for the local paper — interview, pictures, that sort of thing.'

As Jack drove me back to my digs, I was really excited: I

was going to work full-time with a professional dance band in Ireland. The future looked rosy.

I'd love a drink, I thought to myself, but I had no money.

* * *

There were congratulations when I got back to my digs. Marie and I discussed my rent, laundry, key for the front door, use of the kitchen, rules of the house — no food in the room and certainly no women. If I wasn't coming home for the evening meal, I must let her know in advance.

This was new to me. All my life I'd never had to worry about laundry, for instance. At home and at school it had been done for me. Now I had to remember to send my shirts, socks and underwear to the laundry each week.

I was to share my room with Frank Malone, but he had been away rehearsing. When I went up to my room, he jumped up from the bed and grabbed my hand, shaking it violently. 'Well done, Joe, that was brilliant. You certainly made Jack's old piano hum — where did you learn to play like that?'

There were two single beds in the room, two lockers and a wardrobe. It was quite a small room and there were no chairs, so we sat on the beds when we weren't sleeping in them. Lino covered the floor and a window looked out on a small front garden below. The bathroom was downstairs at the end of the hall. There was no heating in our room, which was going to be my home for some time to come.

Frank, who came from Belfast, turned out to be a really great quietly spoken guy. There was only one thing he was interested in: music. We'd be driving to a gig in the wagon, and the rest of the lads would be discussing soccer, hurling, films, women or cars. Frank wanted to talk only about music. He was doing some arrangements for the band and would be scribbling away as we drove along. Naturally as we shared rooms, we would share experiences, often talking into the small hours on nights when we weren't playing.

Frank had a wonderful ear. His taste when I joined the band was strictly jazz, but when he left the band a year later, I'd got him interested in classical music. Meanwhile, he'd got me interested in jazz. He was quite at ease with my blindness right from that first day. He filled me in on the personalities in the band, saying, 'I like Ballina, and I think you'll like it too.'

That night, we went to the pub. Frank had arranged to meet Denis and Aidan the trumpet players, who were both from the North, Denis from Belfast and Aidan from Omagh. As we sat down at the bar, Denis said to me, 'If you're like the rest of us when we joined the band, you'll have no money. Don't worry, we'll buy the drinks tonight and one day you can treat us.'

'You're dead right,' I said, 'I am broke but I'll make it up to you when I get paid.'

Thanks be to God, I'd got a drink.

* * *

The following night was my first gig with the Jack Ruane Band. Frank and I walked to the Town Hall where the dance was to take place. He was carrying his sax in its case. We arrived about half past seven. The stage was reached from the back by a flight of stairs and, as I reached the steps, I realised that there was a group of people hanging around. Frank placed my hand on the banister as instructed, and I walked up to the top, turned left and through the door onto the stage. I walked straight across the stage to the piano. I could feel many eyes on my back — they were all eager to see how I would manage, and as they followed me upstairs I heard one of the group whisper, 'Well, that's one problem solved.' I realised I needed a little chat with these people about my blindness, but I couldn't blame them. I was probably the first blind person they'd ever met.

The band was set up by eight o'clock. They sat on chairs in two rows, the four saxes in front, with the two trumpets, drummer and bass player behind. I was also at the back. In front of each musician was a music stand holding that person's 'library'. This was a large volume of numbered sheet music. Jack would call out the numbers to be played and the musicians would slip through their library and take them out, ready for playing.

When Jack came onto the stage, he walked straight over to me, shook my hand and said, 'Good luck, son, just play the way you did at the audition and everything will be all right.'

Billy the bass player slapped me on the shoulder. 'Okay, lad, give it a good skelp.' This was one of his favourite sayings.

It was only then I met Johnny Bruen, the vocalist, who hadn't been at the audition. He came over and introduced himself. He and Billy were good mates. The banter between them was great to listen to, as they were constantly ribbing each other. Johnny wished me well and told me to take no notice of 'The Taoiseach' as Billy was called.

The band struck up with 'Dancing Time'. The piano was a big, clangy, very loud instrument, but after the first number Jack told me to take the front off and lift up the top. I felt as if I was playing a blacksmith's anvil, but Jack said, 'That's better, now we can hear you. All right, we'll play number ten: 'High Society'. This starts in B flat, Joe, and goes to E flat.'

It was great to be playing with a ten-piece band in Ireland. I wished they could see and hear me at home in Liverpool. The hall began to fill up and after every number the crowd applauded. Johnny Bruen was a fine singer and Tommy Murphy was one of the best drummers I'd heard.

Halfway through the evening, Jack told the band to take a break, except for me, Tommy the drummer and Billy the bass player. We had to stay on and play for ten minutes.

'Play anything you like, Joe,' he said. 'A set of slow foxtrots, a set of quicksteps and a set of old-time waltzes.'

I began to play some sing-along numbers. The crowd sang along as they danced. It was great and the applause was tremendous. At the end of the break, Jack picked up his clarinet and began to play some Benny Goodman numbers. We were swinging now, just Jack and I with the drummer and bass. The crowd went crazy. Jack slapped me on the shoulder — 'God bless you, son, you're fabulous.'

Then the bubble burst. He went to the microphone.

'Ladies and gentlemen, I would like to introduce my new piano player, Joe Bollard.' He dragged me from the piano stool, took my hand and brought me to the front of the stage. I felt awkward. 'And I would like to point out to you, ladies and gentlemen, that Joe is totally blind.'

The applause was deafening but I was furious. 'Isn't he wonderful? A blind man and he can play the piano like that?'

'Jesus, I'll kill him,' I thought.

There was more applause as I returned to the piano with Jack leading me by the hand. The atmosphere built up, the band played brilliantly, the crowd cheered and applauded, but it was spoilt for me — no one was going to make use of my disability as a vehicle to further their own popularity or that of their band.

After the dance, people were milling around and I was the centre of attention. Jack introduced me to lots of people, but I was still angry. We had a photo session with the local newspaper, and I said I didn't think my blindness had anything to do with my playing.

We went back to Jack's house which was full of people, all talking noisily. I asked Jack if I could talk to him privately and we went into his front room.

'Jack, I don't want you to do that ever again,' I began.

'Do what, son?'

'Use my blindness to promote the band, or even to promote me.'

'I don't understand your problem,' he protested.

'I'm a piano player first of all, who just happens to be blind. It's not a miracle. My fingers, hands and feet work okay, my eyes don't work but I don't need them for playing. Don't do it again, Jack. If you do, I'm going back to Liverpool. I want that understood from the start.'

'All right, son. Cool down, it won't happen again.'

That night, as Frank and I lay awake, talking about the evening, I explained about my anger with Jack.

'Well Joe,' he said, 'you must understand, you're the first blind musician most of the people in this town have ever seen, and they feel that everything you do is brave and wonderful.'

'They're going to have to change their thinking,' I said.

'No, Joe. You're going to have to change it for them. Don't let them treat you like a freak.'

Of course he was right and I accepted what he said. I was determined to make a name for myself through my piano playing alone.

~ Twelve ~

'Joe was brilliant last night, he played like Fats Waller.'

'What would you know about Fats Waller, you ignoramus? He never drove a band wagon or played a bass out of tune.'

'My bass isn't out of tune — it just plays the wrong notes. Who cares anyway? The punters don't know — if they did, they'd notice when you sing flat.'

We were on our way to my second gig with the band, which was in Westport, and Billy Quigley and Johnny Bruen were slagging each other as usual. As we drove along in the band wagon, their banter kept us all laughing.

The gig went well, and when Jack introduced me to the crowd he didn't mention that I was blind. My threat must have worked. We played until two in the morning and I was dozing on the way back in the band wagon when I heard the word 'blind'.

I listened and three of the lads were discussing me, saying that Jack shouldn't have taken on a blind person. 'Getting him on and off the stage, taking him to the jacks — he might trip over the mike leads — and when we go on tour, who's going to look after him?'

I wanted to jump up and say, 'Hey, that's me you're talking about,' but I held my tongue. I was determined to show this lot that I could make it even if I was as blind as a bat.

* * *

The following Sunday, Frank told me we were going to a carnival.

'What's that all about?' I asked.

'Playing in a bloody marquee. You'll find out when we get there.'

I discovered that these carnivals were organised by the local GAA club or by a priest as a fund-raising venture. They usually lasted a fortnight. There would be dancing four of five nights a week, and hurling or football matches, all taking place in a local field with a funfair — roundabouts, sideshows, swings, the lot. There would be a huge marquee in the field where the dances were held, with a floor more suited to skiing than dancing. Four great poles down the centre held up the tent.

The sanitation often left much to be desired. Phyllis, our saxophonist, regularly complained about the Ladies at the carnivals. As for the Gents — Billy Quigley told me when I asked him, 'Well, Joe, just point Percy at the bush and hope the bees have other things on their minds.'

When we arrived at my first carnival, which was at some small country place in Co. Galway, we were given a meal of ham and lettuce. This was my fourth gig with the band and three times we'd been given ham and lettuce for our meal.

'If I eat any more bloody lettuce, I'll grow pointed ears,' Billy remarked.

'You mean you haven't noticed?' Johnny Bruen jibed.

The acoustics in the marquees were terrible. It was like playing inside a cardboard box, particularly if there was a strong wind. I used to feel really claustrophobic. There was always a strange smell, a mixture of toilets, paraffin oil and hay. The paraffin was applied lavishly to the floor to make it slippery for dancing, and to my mind it was a tremendous fire hazard. I never smell paraffin today without thinking back to the carnivals and the marquees.

On one occasion when we were playing in a marquee somewhere in the wilds of Mayo, the speakers from our PA system were tightly secured to two of the poles in the middle of the tent. The place was thronged. Jack was playing to the crowd. It was no good playing big band numbers or jazz or even quick-tempo pop numbers in a rural place like this. The dancers wanted old-time waltzes, quicksteps, and slow foxtrots with an Irish flavour.

Shortly before our break, someone shouted, 'Play the "Siege of Ennis"!' I had no idea what they wanted, but the shout was taken up by some more people.

Jack went to the microphone and said, 'We're not a céilí band, we don't play céilí music.'

'Play the "Siege of Ennis"!' The shouts grew louder and more insistent.

Jack was adamant, coming up with a great get-out clause. 'There's not enough space in the marquee for a "Siege of Ennis". It's not suitable for set dancing.'

Then a huge farmer stepped forward and grabbed Jack by the lapels. 'If you don't play the "Siege of Ennis", I'll go and pull those two little grannyphones off the poles and shove them where they won't fit.'

Jack picked up his alto sax and turned to the drummer shouting, 'Tommy, play a reel. Joe, just vamp on the piano, try to follow me.'

Jack amazed me. He belted out a reel on the saxophone no problem. Tommy Murphy could play anything on the drums. But as for me — I just played umpa-umpa on the piano, trying to get the right chords in behind Jack. I had no idea what I was playing and neither had Billy. The crowd went berserk, charging up and down the marquee, shrieking and yelling. This went on for about ten minutes. When we stopped, exhausted, the applause was deafening.

'Well done, Bollard, you certainly skelped it that time,' said Billy. 'We'll make a céilí musician of you yet.'

We played at a lot of carnivals that summer, but I never liked the idea of playing in a marquee. The band never sounded good and some of the pianos I had to play were straight out of the Ark. Often they had candle holders on the front, and sometimes actual candles, which I would light, just for laughs. Another time, we pulled a dead rat out of the bottom of the piano. Billy joked that it was left over from a local musical production of *The Pied Piper*.

* * *

Summer changed to autumn. The carnivals were over, and we moved back into the dancehalls. The band was sounding good and I was taking a great interest in jazz, with Frank as my tutor. We would borrow the key of the Town Hall on Saturday afternoons and spend hours trying out different ideas — he on the tenor sax and I on the clangy piano. There was no heating on during the day, so we would emerge from our practice numb with cold, but excited and happy. I was learning from Frank all the time, mainly about chord structure. Having been trained as a classical musician, my ability to improvise was almost non-existent. Frank would read to me at night from various music books he had, and we'd listen to records played on an old record player I'd bought from one of the lads in the band.

In the evenings, I'd go to the pub and get drunk. Earning more meant that I drank more, and as a single man living in digs, I had few expenses. Not many people knew about my drink problem as I was good at hiding it. I drank a lot alone in my room, and when I was drunk I would fall into bed and sleep it off. Marie Flynn thought I was making up for the hours spent travelling with the band. I think her husband Jim knew, but he never said anything — he was quite a heavy drinker himself. Most nights, Frank would bring me home very drunk and, although he tried to get me to cut down on my drinking, it just got worse. He put up with a lot from me.

As Christmas approached, we were preparing for the North Mayo Hunt Ball, to be held in Enniscrone on St Stephen's Day. This was an annual event — a dress dance with the ladies in long evening dresses and the men in dress suits. We rehearsed the 'hunting medley', a selection of tunes straight out of 'Merrie England'.

I had been feeling depressed over Christmas, and on St Stephen's Day had spent quite some time drinking in my room, thinking about my family in Liverpool. When the band wagon called for me, I was already drunk but managed to hide it.

On stage, we got ourselves together. I sat at the useless piano whose sustain pedal didn't work, listening as Jack issued instructions about keeping tempo correct and not playing too loudly. Then he turned to me. 'Joe, keep your eye on this bottle of brandy. It's been given to the band for the break.'

This caused laughter in the band and he gave me the bottle, which I placed under the piano, at the same time trying to prise out the cork. Sitting at the back, I knew that nobody would see my efforts to get the cork out. As we played, I struggled with it and eventually got it out with a great pop, spilling some of the contents. That didn't matter to me, and as we played on, I was swigging brandy from the bottle. Nobody was looking at me — they were too busy watching the talent cavorting in front of the stage.

After two hours, the break came. 'Okay lads, brandy time,' said Jack. I tried to stand up and I remember nothing more. I collapsed on the stage with almost all the brandy inside me.

I woke the next day, at home in bed, wishing I was dead. I felt dreadful. There was a basin by the bed into which I immediately threw up. I could smell food being cooked downstairs and my stomach heaved again. My head was bursting, my throat on fire. I lay there wanting to die. Jim Flynn came into the room.

'Who's a pretty boy then?' he joked. 'You've done it this time, young man.'

He told me that I had frightened the life out of people when I collapsed. Only when the brandy bottle was found was my 'indiscretion' discovered.

'Practically a whole bottle of brandy — God bless you and all who sail in you. The boys are after your blood — it probably contains most of their brandy.' He laughed at his own joke.

We weren't playing that night, so I slept for twelve hours. Frank came in and told me that there would be an inquest on my behaviour when we met for the gig the following day. He said that Jack hadn't said much about the brandy incident but the lads were furious with me.

As for me, I didn't care tuppence about their bloody brandy. I'd get drunk again the next night — sod the lot of them!

* * *

We were playing locally the next day, and Jack called us all together when we had set up our instruments. I had been drinking that day and, although not drunk, I was pretty high.

'Joe, that wasn't at all clever of you in Enniscrone,' said Jack. 'You let the band down very badly. The committee gave the brandy to be shared out among the band. It was very mean of you. You've let your friends down big time.'

I wasn't paying any attention.

'We had to say you'd been taken ill when you collapsed on stage,' he continued. It seemed that I had been taken home and put to bed by a neighbour.

'This will have to stop, Joe,' Jack warned. 'You're letting yourself and the boys down. We'll overlook it this time, but if it happens again, there'll be trouble.'

I felt no remorse. I would drink when and where I liked, I thought. I didn't need lectures from this culchie.

The following day I went to the pub with five or six lads and we decided to have a drinking competition. Each of us put a pound in the middle of the table. We were to drink only pints, and the one who could drink the most without getting sick would win the money. I never drank pints, only shorts — mainly whiskey — but I was willing to give it a try.

If you got sick, you were eliminated. So if you went to the Gents, you had to be accompanied by one of the others. As the evening wore on, people dropped out of the contest, one by one, until there was just myself and one other guy left. We had to buy our own pints. We were level at nineteen each. We ordered another pint each, but suddenly the other guy fell across the table and was violently sick.

I had won. I picked up the money gleefully, having drunk almost two and a half gallons of beer, just for a bet.

I walked home with a friend, and fell asleep on my bed for three hours. Then Marie Flynn called me downstairs where a party was in full swing. The house was full of people and I was really drunk but I immediately took over the party. I began to sing but had to stop because I couldn't remember the words.

Then Marie said, 'Joe, I'd like you to meet Sarah. She's from Dublin but she's living in Ballina.'

'I'm delighted to meet you, Sarah,' I said. 'It's good to meet someone from Dublin.'

I have forgotten the rest of the evening, but I know that I went to bed and threw up out the bedroom window, to the utter disgust of Marie Flynn and her guests.

I was hardly sober for the next week. The band was playing most nights, but I managed to hide from Jack the state I was in, though the lads were well aware of it.

On Sunday, we left Ballina early as we were playing in Donegal town that night. I felt dreadful and everyone said that I looked terrible. I said I thought I was coming down with Asian flu, which was reaching epidemic proportions in Ireland at the time.

I drank half a bottle of whiskey before the dance that night. When we started to play, I thought the band sounded rather strange. I couldn't hear properly — everything sounded far away. Then I felt this dreadful pain, just as if someone was clawing at my guts. I opened my mouth to scream but no sound came out.

Then I collapsed.

* * *

I don't remember what happened next, but apparently I was carried off stage while Jack told the dancers that I had Asian flu. I was laid out in the back seat of the band wagon and brought home to Ballina where I lay in bed for three days while Marie Flynn nursed me. At last she was so worried that she sent for the doctor.

The doctor examined me from head to toe, then he sat down on my bed and asked, 'How old are you?'

'Twenty-two.'

'Well, I'm not the kind of person to pull any punches, and if you keep on the way you're going, you won't see twenty-three.'

He told me that I was drinking myself to death, that I was in a shocking state. 'Your heart won't take much more, and God knows what your liver is like,' he continued. I knew he was serious: I had never felt so ill in my life.

'Do you want to live?' he asked.

All I could do was nod my head.

'Okay, I'll tell you what we'll do. I'll get Jack to give you a month off work. You stay in bed until you get stronger. I'll visit you every day and I'll give you a course of medication to help you, but it won't be easy. I'll speak to Mrs Flynn and your friend Frank — between us we may be able to fight it, but the toughest part lies with you, Joe. You've got to *want* to stop drinking. Will you give it a try?'

Again, I just nodded.

The next month was horrific. The hallucinations were awful: I felt as though a metal hand was clawing out my stomach, I thought rats were running over my face. I had the shakes. At least the longing for a drink became weaker and weaker as the month progressed. But I had dreadful nightmares and my head was filled with noises. I think perhaps the fact that I couldn't see the rats and snakes of my imaginings made it worse for me. And the noises in my head were shattering. There were screams in my head — piercing screams, clanging, jangling, then the screams again. I couldn't bear it, and added my own screams to the ones that were tormenting me. I prayed to God, I cursed God, I wanted to die. I screamed out every filthy word I knew, every obscenity, and this was totally out of character. And all the time, there were tears ... I could never endure that month again. I had heard of hell on earth and I now knew what it meant. I went through it.

The doctor was wonderful, visiting as often as he could. Marie and Jim were fantastic — I know I disturbed their sleep many a night with my screaming and roaring. Fortunately for Frank, he was away for much of that month, and by the time I had recovered, he had left the band. Musicians come and go. After Frank left, I never shared my room with anyone for long.

I came through the hell of that month, thanks to the doctor, thanks to Marie and Jim Flynn, but most of all, thanks to the Man Above.

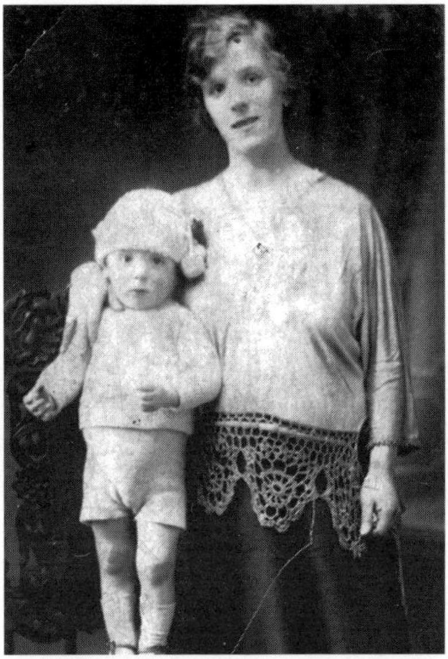

Left: Joe's mother with her first-born, Richard (Dickie). In 1948, Dickie was killed in the Middle East while serving with the British Army.

Below: Joe with three of his sisters (L to R) Vera, Maggie and Sue.

Above: Geography Lesson at St Vincent's School for the Blind in West Derby. Joe is pictured fourth from right, standing at the globe. Sister Joseph is on the left.

Left: Joe with the Braille award he won five years in a row, while a pupil at St Vincent's.

Left: 'I said it was only my eyes didn't work!' Joe at home in Liverpool.

Below: Joe (seated at piano) indulges his early passion for music, together with classmates.

Above: Happy Days! The Jack Ruane Band. Joe is standing on the extreme right with a guitar. *Below*: Wedding Bells! Joe and Sarah with Jack and Maura Ruane.

Above: The Dalkey Island Hotel: Joe (second from right) with owner Jim Delaney (centre) who has just been crowned King of Dalkey.

Right: Joe and Sarah after Joe's election as Lord Mayor of Bray, 1981.

Above: Joe cues another record at BLB in 1979.

Below: Relaxing at the piano.

Right: The Bollard sons: (L to R) Noel, Declan and Joseph on Declan's wedding day.

Below: Joe sets off for a round of golf with Declan.

Above: The Blazing Saddles: Joe and Nick Eoghan stop for a break, California, March 1992.

Below: One man and his dog: Joe and Whiskey, July 1997.

~ Thirteen ~

A little over three weeks after my collapse on the stage in Donegal, I got up and came down to the living room, where I sat by the fire and really felt I had come back into the world.

Jack Ruane came to see me that night, and he was crying as he said, 'Well done, son — keep it going and we'll all help you. We've missed you in the band. Come back when you're good and ready.'

It was another ten days or so before I was back to some kind of health. I was still very shaky, but I was eating well, sleeping without nightmares and beginning to feel a lot better.

The day before I returned to the band, I went to the parish priest and took the Pledge. He wanted me to take it for a probationary period of twelve months, but I insisted that I wanted it for life. He gave me a Pioneer pin, and I rather sheepishly put it in my lapel.

The next day, the band wagon called at the digs for me. We were playing in Limerick. Shortly before we left Ballina, Jack, who was driving, turned and addressed us all in the back of the wagon. 'I'd like to welcome Joe back to the band and I just want to say two things. If I catch Joe drinking on the stage again, I'll sack him on the spot, and also, if I catch anyone giving him a drink on stage, I'll sack that person as well. Well done, son, it's good to have you back.'

The lads in the band were great. There were one or two comments about my Pioneer pin, but most of the talk was about our forthcoming English tour. It was 1958 and, in those days, the bishops in the rural areas of Ireland didn't permit dancing in Lent. So for six weeks, we were deprived of work in our own country. This meant a trip to Britain for work.

Interestingly, however, there was dancing in Dublin, and I often thought it ridiculous that dancing was a sin in the country but okay for the Catholics in the capital city!

* * *

Shortly after my return to the band, Johnny Bruen left. We were without a vocalist and had a big dance coming up in Galway, so Jack offered some of the vocal numbers to me. I said I'd give it a go, offering to sing the slow numbers; Tommy, our drummer, would sing the quicker numbers. Jack was delighted with my efforts — it saved him from having to pay another vocalist — and we started to rehearse our 'English programme'.

We would be appearing in Irish clubs throughout England, so we would be playing mostly Irish numbers. I already knew a lot of Irish songs, which we used to sing at home, gathered around the fire.

The week before we left, Jack advertised in the national papers for two vocalists. He felt that we needed a male and a female singer for this tour. 'You can sing the slow ballads, Joe, but I want someone for the up-tempo numbers — give them a bit of life,' Jack said. He brought me to Dublin to do the auditions with him.

The auditions were held in Barry's Hotel over a period of two days. We stayed in the hotel and I accompanied dozens of singers. Jack would discuss each one with me after we had heard them. We chose a female vocalist the first day: a pleasant Dublin girl, Maureen Lally. She had a lovely clear voice, sort of plaintive — just right for singing Irish songs to Irish people in England.

The male applicants weren't great. We had almost given up hope when, on the last day, a young lad came in. 'I've come for the audition mentioned in the paper,' he said shyly.

'Okay, son, what do you want to sing?' Jack asked.

'"Mac the Knife".'

I did a swinging introduction. He was brilliant: he had a wonderful sense of timing, a sort of jazz feel about his delivery. He sang two more numbers. His name was Michael O'Sullivan, and although we didn't realise it, we had just auditioned somebody who would be one of the most popular singers ever with the Jack Ruane Band.

Mick, as he preferred to be called, travelled back with us to Ballina. He had no luggage — just the clothes he stood up in. He was from Thurles and, like most of us when we joined the band, completely broke. Maureen Lally stayed in Dublin and joined us later for the English tour.

On the way back to Ballina, I told Mick about the band, the personnel, the type of music we played and the forthcoming English trip. 'How old are you, Mick?' I asked, thinking he seemed very young to be joining a band.

'Just gone eighteen,' he replied. 'I've sung with a few semi-pro bands but I want to make it with a big band. That's why I applied. What's the Head like?' He meant Jack.

'He's okay. Just don't overdo the drinking and you'll be all right,' I warned.

Poor Mick — the drink was his big problem.

* * *

A few weeks before our trip to Dublin, we were playing one night in Ballina. After the dance, Tommy, our drummer, told me, 'There's a girl been sitting in front of the stage all night, just looking up at you. She didn't dance at all — just kept her eyes on you. You're all right there, boy.'

'Well, she can forget it, I'm not interested in women.'

The following week we were playing in a small dancehall not far away, and the lads told me that the same girl was there again, just looking up at me all night.

On Sunday we were playing in Enniscrone, and Tommy told me that she was there again, just looking at me. 'I'll find out her name,' he volunteered.

'You needn't bother,' I replied.

After the dance, I was sitting beside the stage when a female voice beside me said, 'Hello, Joe, do you remember me? I'm Sarah. I was at the party at Marie Flynn's house just after Christmas.'

'Hello again, Sarah,' I said nonchalantly. 'I believe you've been following the band around for the last few weeks. Let me tell you right from the start, Sarah, I'm not the slightest bit interested in women, I've too much to do, working with the band.'

Everywhere we played locally, Sarah turned up for the next few weeks. Then, one particular night we weren't playing and I went with some of the lads from our band to hear a very good band that was playing in the town hall. While I was sitting listening to the band, I was surprised to feel a hand on my shoulder. 'Hello, Joe, it's me, Sarah. This is a ladies' choice — would you care to dance?'

I shuffled around the floor for a while, then sat down again and somehow began to chat, first about the band, then about each other. She seemed very relaxed and didn't seem to have any problems with my blindness, and we danced again. At the end of the night, she said, 'I suppose with you being blind, I'll have to walk you home. I know where you live, so that won't be too difficult.'

We walked home and when we reached the gate she said, 'How do you feel about going for a walk on Thursday afternoon? I know you're not playing because I made it my business to find out. About three o'clock then?' She was gone.

On Thursday afternoon, Sarah called for me. We went for a long walk and I listened as she told me her life story. She also came from a large family. Born in Ringsend in Dublin, both of her parents had died when she was very young, and she had been placed in an orphanage. On leaving the orphanage, she had had one or two jobs and was now living with her sister in Ballina, looking after her sister's children, and generally keeping house.

She liked Ballina, had never had a boyfriend and admitted that she was attracted to me. She liked my singing and playing but it wasn't anything to do with that. She mentioned the famous party in Marie Flynn's house and seemed glad when I told her I no longer drank.

It was a pleasant afternoon, and I quite enjoyed her company. We shared a lot of experiences, both of us having been educated in convents. We'd both been reared in Dublin too, and her Dublin accent appealed to me, as it reminded me of my early childhood.

We went to the Astoria Cinema the following Monday, to

see *The Glenn Miller Story*. I actually kissed her goodnight that night, and we agreed to meet the following Thursday.

I saw quite a lot of Sarah during the next couple of weeks. The night before we left for our English tour, she begged me to come back to Ballina when the tour was over. I had said that I might stay and look for work in London. I didn't make any firm promise to Sarah but said that I'd write to her when I was away. I could do this as I had a portable typewriter.

* * *

We left Ballina very early in the morning to catch the Liverpool boat, travelling in the band wagon. The crossing was dreadfully rough and stormy. I didn't get sick, but many of the other passengers did, including Mick, who had come to be called 'Covey'. Jack had begun to call him this, and the name had stuck.

I was sharing a cabin with Covey that night. He arrived in the cabin at around one o'clock, as pissed as a newt. I had chosen the bottom bunk and was half asleep. He undressed, piddled in the handbasin, told me I was the greatest blind person he'd ever met and that he loved me; then when trying to climb up to the top bunk, he put his smelly foot right on my face. The ship lurched at that moment, sending him sprawling across the cabin.

'Let me out, I'll walk!' he shouted at the top of his voice, laughing loudly at his own stupidity.

Someone banged on the wall of the cabin next door.

'Piss off and go to sleep!' Covey shouted, then began to sing 'Mac the Knife' as loud as he could.

He puked all over the cabin floor in the night, cursing the ship for lurching. I didn't sleep at all and was wrecked when we docked in Liverpool. But Covey was one of those people you couldn't get really angry with: he was a silly, lovable, funny, annoying person, with a tremendous sense of humour.

* * *

I stayed in Liverpool while the rest of the band headed off for Manchester where we were to be based for the first four days of the tour.

It was great to be home again and I was greeted like the

prodigal son, although I had been absent for less than a year and had telephoned home nearly every week. My mother thought I looked thin and my father wanted to know all about the culchies, the fishing in the River Moy, and the places I'd visited.

When I told him that I'd played in almost every county in Ireland, he was really taken aback. 'You mean you travel all over the country in a van, playing music?'

'Yes, and getting paid for it.'

Later, I caused quite a sensation when I was invited out to the pub and told the family I didn't want to go as I no longer drank. They were simply astounded.

I didn't tell them about my ordeal — simply that I was off it since Christmas or thereabouts.

'Thanks be to God, my prayers have been answered,' said my mother.

Our first gig in England was in Liverpool. Unlike all the other gigs we were booked for, this one wasn't in an Irish club but in a parochial hall down on the Scotland Road, which was a really tough quarter of Liverpool. The priest who was running it told us as we were setting up our gear that he didn't think many people would come to the dance as he hadn't done much advertising. He was right. There were actually seventeen people at the dance, and eleven of those got in for nothing because they were members of my family and their friends!

Jack used this fiasco as a rehearsal for the tour proper, but he was quite angry with the priest. After the dance, I went home with my family and we sat up into the night while I answered questions about my life as a band musician. I told my mother about Sarah.

'I hope she's a good Catholic girl, Joe,' she said.

'Yes, Mum. Sarah is a good Catholic — she goes to Mass regularly.'

'Well, it looks as if your going to Ireland was a good move after all.'

* * *

I took the train from Lime Street Station the following day and headed for Manchester to join the rest of the band. I would be seeing my family again in six weeks' time on the way home.

The following three nights, we played in an Irish club in Manchester. This was my first experience of playing for Irish emigrants. There was a resident band in the club, which, according to English union rules, had to play for an hour and a half before any visiting band. Covey and I were really taken with this band — they were playing a lot of the pop music of the day, and they had a guitar player, something only just coming into vogue in Ireland. They also played rock and roll, the new music of the 1950s. Covey knew the words to a lot of the numbers and we'd talk for hours about Elvis Presley, Little Richard, Gene Vincent and Eddy Cochrane. The English stars of the day included Cliff Richard, Billy Furey and Tommy Steele.

After our stint in Manchester, we moved on to Derby and then to Birmingham. In both, the clubs were packed to capacity with crowds coming to hear the Jack Ruane Band from Ballina.

I was doing a lot more singing now, and when we got to Birmingham, there was that poster again:

THE JACK RUANE BAND
FEATURING BLIND VOCALIST AND PIANIST
JOE BOLLARD

Jack apologised at once: 'It's nothing to do with me, son. The local papers got hold of it and are using it — I swear it's not my fault.'

I finished singing 'The Old Bog Road'. The crowd went wild, and Jack brought me to the front of the stage when the applause had died down.

'Ladies and gentlemen, this is Joe Bollard,' he began. 'As you have heard, he is a wonderful singer and plays piano brilliantly, but he is adamant that you appreciate his talent for what it is, and at no time must you allow his blindness to influence your appreciation of his ability.'

I didn't know quite how to take this — I felt that it was a subtle way of using my blindness to further the popularity of the band, but Jack swore that it wasn't, so I gave him the benefit of the doubt.

* * *

It was Jack's job to find us digs when we were on tour. In Birmingham, we stayed in a big old house with large rooms. After the gig, we sat up late, playing poker. I had learned to play poker some months earlier, while travelling in the band wagon. Of course, I used Braille cards. It's possible for a blind person to play with sighted people, using these special cards which have Braille on the corners. I wouldn't deal, as a good Braille reader can read the cards as they are dealing.

The five of us who were playing were sitting on the floor around a gas fire. At about three o'clock in the morning, when the game was at its most exciting, there was a 'pop' from the fire and it went out.

'Who's got a shilling for the bloody fire?' someone said.

But nobody wanted to put his money in the meter. We didn't want to stop playing either, but without a fire the place would be freezing. Then I had an idea.

I always carried a 'style', a small instrument rather like a punch or awl, for writing Braille. I had been taught by my brothers when I was very young how to pick a lock. I found the padlock on the gas meter and, using my style, I picked the lock, emptied out all the coins, fastened the lock, and fed all the coins back into the meter. We had enough heat to last us as long as we liked, and we could finish our game. I dread to think what the landlady's gas bill was like, and how she explained the shortfall in the amount when the man came to read the meter.

From Birmingham, we moved on to Luton, where there was a huge Irish population — most of the men working in the motor industry — and from Luton to London.

We stayed in London for a fortnight, using it as a base, playing in Watford, Northampton, Reading and of course in a number of Irish clubs in London itself. My favourite was the Gresham Ballroom with its revolving stage. It was in a different class from the other Irish clubs, reminding me of the Grafton Ballroom and the Locarno Ballroom in Liverpool.

I was amazed at the popularity of the band. All through the tour, crowds turned out to hear and see us and we played to packed halls everywhere. Liverpool was the only bad night we had on the whole tour.

During our London stay, we played at the Banba Club in Cricklewood, once again to huge crowds. Afterwards, I was approached by the manager of the club, who offered me a job as vocalist with the resident band. This would mean working with the band three nights a week, but only as a vocalist, as they already had a very good pianist. He offered more money than Jack was paying me.

I told him that we were travelling up north for a week, but when we returned to London at the end of the tour I would let him know. During the tour, I was writing quite regularly to Sarah, and I telephoned her a number of times, but I didn't mention the offer to her. In fact, I told nobody about it as I wanted to make the decision on my own and not be influenced by anybody.

* * *

From London, we moved on to Leeds, where I had been before — for the game at Elland Road between Leeds United and Everton. Everton lost, so it wasn't a place with happy memories, but this occasion would leave me with better ones.

Covey often read the paper to me while we were travelling, and on the way up, in the band wagon, he read the racing page to me. Like me, he was interested in horse racing. When we got to Leeds, I put my last ten shillings on a horse. I was flat broke. Most of the band heard what I had done and they followed suit, placing bets from a pound to a fiver. To my delight, the horse won at 25/1. I was rich, and so was the rest of the band. The lads thought I could do that sort of thing every day, but I told them that backing horses without due study was a mug's game.

Using Leeds as our base, we played in Huddersfield, Sheffield and in Manchester again. All the time, I was thinking about the offer from the Banba Club manager.

We were heading back to London for the last week of the tour when I decided not to take the job. It would be great to live and work in London, but although I would earn more money, I would spend more just trying to live.

To be honest, I really wanted to get back to Ireland, to Ballina and to Sarah. That night, I phoned to tell her that I was coming back with the band and that I had decided to stay.

~ Fourteen ~

We spent the last week of the English tour in London, playing in the Blarney, the Gresham, and at Watford, ending with a huge farewell dance on Sunday night at the Banba.

I told the manager that I wasn't taking the job, and he seemed disappointed, even increasing his offer, but I wasn't tempted. He said that if I ever changed my mind, I would always be welcome at the Banba Club.

Instead of sounding tired after such a strenuous tour, the band sounded really great that night. We were all looking forward to getting home, and we were really swinging — the crowd shouted and yelled for more. I did a big ballad version of 'Love Thee Dearest', which brought the house down. Phyllis had to do her sax solo 'Danny Boy' three times.

After the dance, at about two o'clock on Monday morning, we packed the band wagon and headed off on the long drive to Liverpool, saying a sad goodbye to Billy Quigley who had decided to stay in England. I heard that he died not long afterwards.

We arrived in Liverpool about breakfast time on Monday morning, and we all headed for the nearest chemist's shop. In those days, contraception was strictly forbidden by the Catholic Church in Ireland, and condoms were unobtainable. The chemist must have thought we were a randy lot when six of us swept into his shop and bought up his entire stock of French letters at half a crown for a packet of three. We could sell them in Ballina for ten shillings each! Of course we had to get them through the customs first — I put my stock of sixteen packets inside my underpants. It was uncomfortable but I got away with it, and I sold every one in Ballina, making a financial kill.

As the boat didn't leave until ten o'clock at night, I spent the rest of the day at home in Spencer Street, where the family pulled my leg about my Irish accent.

The family was breaking up now: Margaret was living in Kirby with her husband Pat, and their children; Sue was in Grove Street with her husband, Johnny, and their family; only God knew where Georgie was; Paddy lived upstairs in our house with his wife, Inez, and their children; Billy was with the army in Hong Kong; Vera had moved to Birmingham. Only my parents and younger brother Ronnie were left.

I was sad about this. I had always felt safe when we were all together in Spencer Street. We had our differences, but we loved each other and were a close-knit bunch, especially when we were young. This bond was strongest among the members of the family who had been left behind when my parents emigrated. They were together for one of their brief spells at that time, although they were soon to separate again. I did see the whole family together again once more, when Sarah and I visited Liverpool later that year.

I had a strange feeling when I left that night that I wasn't just taking leave of my parents, but saying goodbye to the whole family, even though they weren't there. As the taxi bumped over the cobblestones of Spencer Street, heading for the pier head and the boat, I remember thinking that sometimes it's a pity we have to grow up.

* * *

We arrived back in Ballina on Tuesday evening, shattered from travelling and looking forward to a few days off. Jack told us that there would be a practice — his name for rehearsals — on Saturday afternoon at his house.

I was now sure that I wanted to remain in Ballina. Yes, I had been missing Sarah, but at that time, I was very raw — I was just off the drink, after all. I think I needed some sort of support, but I didn't want commitment. I had learned from my earlier experience with Vera. I had no reservations about the Jack Ruane Band, though: I loved the work and was eager to make my home in Ballina so that I could be with the band.

I had enjoyed meeting my family again, but I would have

been reluctant to settle in Liverpool. I would have been tempted, I felt, to start drinking again.

On Wednesday, I contacted Sarah and we arranged to go for a walk the following day. It was a lovely day in early spring and we walked for quite some time. I was full of chat about the English tour, but didn't tell her about the job I had been offered in London. I later discovered that she too had been offered a job, as a priest's housekeeper somewhere down the country, but had turned it down when she heard I was coming back to Ballina.

We went to the pictures that evening and when she left me back at my digs I kissed her and told her that I was getting very fond of her. Sarah said that she felt the same way. I was glad, but I knew that if we were to get serious about each other, we would need to have a long chat. I decided to let it wait and see how things developed.

* * *

It was back to business as usual with the band, and on Easter Sunday we played at Ballincollig. I remember that there was a dreadful fight during the dance and the guards were called. We had experienced trouble during our English tour but it was unusual for an Irish dancehall at that time. I was glad when it was over.

During the next few months there were changes in the band. Frank Malone was now with a band in Belfast. I missed him as we were good friends and he was a great help and encouragement to me. We kept in touch for many years. A new bass player replaced Billy; our second trumpet player returned home to Omagh, and Jack's young son, Jud, joined us on second trumpet. He was no more than thirteen, and Jack only used him on gigs in Ballina and at local dances. Even at that early age he was good and showed great promise.

A new word had crept into the vocabulary of the dancing public at this time: 'showband'. The dance orchestras were rapidly disappearing and being replaced by groups of musicians who no longer sat down to play. A lot of their material was 'busked' (played by ear without music), guitars were in vogue — bass, lead and rhythm. The musicians indulged in fancy steps on stage, and some wore outlandish clothes. They played 'cover' versions of the pop music of the day. Most of all, they played rock and roll, and country and western music. Musical tastes were changing all over the world and Ireland, although a little behind, was no different.

Television was now being received in Ireland from Britain — mainly on the east coast and in Northern Ireland; shows like *Juke Box Jury* and *Six-Five Special* were influencing the music scene. Many, though not all, of the showbands, were 'co-op', meaning that they had no specific leader or owner of the band. All the money they earned was pooled and shared equally, as opposed to the regular dance bands run by a band leader who paid each musician a set wage. Bands such as the Johnny Quigley Showband, the Clipper Carlton Showband, and the Premier Aces were beginning to make it big — they were drawing in the crowds. New dancehalls were being built — huge buildings, with room for thousands of dancers. More and more people wanted to hear the new phenomenon.

Tommy Murphy our drummer, Covey and I were ardent showband enthusiasts and, whenever we had the chance, we would hire a car and travel, sometimes a long distance, to hear them. When travelling in the band wagon, we would talk about their sound and the ideas they were putting to music.

Jack, however, was totally against the showband idea. 'They won't last, son,' he would say to me. 'This rock and roll is a passing phase which is due out soon. These buskers aren't musicians at all, just chancers, mark my words.'

But everywhere we played, at some stage, the dancers would shout, 'Play some rock and roll!' 'Give us some Elvis!' Afterwards they would say to us, 'You haven't got a guitar player' or 'You're good, but don't you think you're a little old-fashioned?'

We were back into the season of carnivals again. One night at a carnival, when things were going extra well and I was getting a lot of personal applause, I was greeted by a woman who asked if I remembered her. As it isn't easy to remember every voice you hear, I had no idea and said so.

'I'm Margaret,' she said. 'I was with you on the boat from England. Do you remember me saying we'd meet again when you were famous? Well, here I am.'

'Hardly famous,' I said, but she insisted that I must be. We talked for a few minutes, then she was gone, and I didn't meet her again.

Another night, at a carnival in Glenamaddy, I suggested to Covey that instead of me playing sing-along numbers on the piano during the break, we might suggest to Jack that we try a few rock and roll numbers, just as an experiment. We put the idea to Tommy, our drummer, and Ronnie the bass player.

Jack reluctantly agreed and we chose 'Twenty Flight Rock', 'Blue Jean Bop' and 'Beebop-alula'. Covey did the singing, I played Jerry Lee Lewis-style piano, Tommy really rocked on the drums, Ronnie pounded out a solid beat on the bass — it was sensational. Covey gyrated on the stage, and the girls screamed at his every movement. We had to do the same three numbers again. That night in Glenamaddy was a turning point for the Jack Ruane Band.

* * *

I had been seeing Sarah as often as possible in my spare time, and we had grown very fond of each other. On my nights off, if we didn't go to the cinema, I would spend the evening with her, babysitting in her sister's house. It was obvious to both of us now that we were in love.

One Saturday morning, I asked Jack's daughter Phyllis to accompany me to a jeweller's in Ballina, where I bought an engagement ring. Phyllis and I were really good friends and I valued her opinion. She often helped me with my shopping, particularly when we were on tour. I asked her to keep the ring a secret from the rest of the band, and she did.

For days I had thought about nothing else. Would Sarah want to be married to a blind man? A blind man working in a band, not knowing where I might finish up working, or where we might have to live.

It requires a special sort of person to be married to someone with a disability. Apart from the obvious physical understanding, there is the psychological understanding. Most important of all is a real understanding of the needs of the partner with the disability.

On 17 May 1958, I suggested to Sarah that we go for a walk. It was a lovely warm day and we went up through the fields surrounding Belleek Castle, a derelict building, once a sanatorium and now a hotel. We sat on a low wall, behind which, believe it or not, a pig was burrowing in the ground, snuffling and snorting. It was like something in a stage-Irish film. We sat talking for a while.

I asked Sarah whether she had ever thought of becoming a nun.

She replied that it had crossed her mind at one time but she had decided against it.

'I'm glad you didn't,' I said.

'Why?'

'Well, nuns can't get married.'

'What do you mean, Joe?'

I produced the ring from my pocket. 'Sarah, I want to marry you. Will you have me? I know it will be difficult for you being married to a blind man, but I'll try my best for you and for us. What do you think of the idea?'

I put the ring on her finger. It was a strange moment. The pig was grunting behind us.

Sarah kissed me and started to cry. 'Yes, Joe, I will marry you.'

We decided to wait eighteen months before getting married. I knew that I would have to start saving, and we put our names on the council housing list for a flat or house.

I left all the planning to Sarah. As her parents were dead, her sister said that she would give us the reception as a wedding present. I insisted on a quiet wedding, and that only immediate family and friends would be invited.

* * *

During that summer, the band was going from strength to strength in popularity. Jack was allowing us to play more rock and roll. However, in many of the dancehalls — particularly those run by priests — rock and roll was forbidden. Often there would be a notice in the hall:

ROCK AND ROLL, JIVING AND CLOSE DANCING
STRICTLY FORBIDDEN

This kind of dancing was looked on as an occasion of sin. I thought and still think this attitude stupid.

One afternoon in early August, Sarah came hurrying around to see me at my digs.

'Joe, I've heard of a vacant flat in Teeling Street,' she said. 'It's not in great condition, but if we take it we'll have the chance of getting a place from the council. What do you think?'

We had a look at the place and it was in a bad state but I could see Sarah's point of view. We agreed to take the flat and we decided that, if we were going to pay rent for it, we might as well live in it. In those days, not many couples lived together as they do today, so there was only one answer — to get married as soon as possible. We agreed that the wedding would be on 16 September, just over a month away.

Of course, when the news got out that we were bringing our wedding forward by a year, everyone thought the obvious, and countless times I had to say, 'No, Sarah isn't pregnant' or 'No, we haven't *got* to get married.' I asked Jack for two weeks off early in September, and Sarah and I went to see the priest.

When he learned that Sarah's surname was the same as my mother's maiden name — Scanlan — he said that we would have to wait while he made enquiries about the possibility that we might be related, but a few days later, he told us that everything was fine.

He then actually tried to dissuade Sarah from going ahead with the marriage. His attitude towards me was pathetic, treating me like a child, talking patronisingly to me, patting my shoulder. However, Sarah took no nonsense from him.

'Joe and I have discussed this at length, Father. I know very well what I'm doing. Joe is quite a capable person, as good as, if not better than, a lot of people that have their sight.'

As with many weddings at that time, ours was a morning affair, starting with eight o'clock mass at St Muirdach's Cathedral. The celebrant was Canon McDonald, later to be made a bishop.

Of course Sarah was late — it was almost a quarter past eight when she finally arrived. As I waited in the church, the canon was becoming impatient.

'If she doesn't come soon, I'll have to start without her,' he said.

Flippantly I replied, 'Well, Father, I hope I won't have to do that tonight.'

My best man, Sarah's brother Michael, told me that if looks could kill I was dead.

As the photographs were being taken outside the church, we heard two old ladies discussing us behind our backs. 'She's only marrying him for publicity because he's in a band, and anyway, who in their right mind would marry a blind man?'

I was going to turn on them but Sarah said, 'Leave them, Joe, they're not worth it.'

Our wedding reception was held in O'Dowd's pub — a small reception with about thirty guests. My mother had come from Liverpool for the wedding but she was the only one of my family present. We would have another little reception in Liverpool, where we were to spend our honeymoon. We took the one o'clock train to Dublin and boarded the boat for Liverpool that night, arriving early the following morning.

Shortly before we left Ballina, Jack had asked me whether I could return earlier than planned as we had an important gig with Ruby Murray. I reluctantly agreed.

Sarah's first impression of Liverpool, was that everyone had a long face, nobody was smiling. A possible explanation may have been that it was early and most people were going to work. Traffic was heavy, lots of people were rushing around.

Everyone in my family was delighted to meet Sarah. Discreetly, they asked me whether she was pregnant, because of the rushed wedding, but I assured them that she wasn't. Our honeymoon was spent at 55 Spencer Street, my childhood home, and I felt good about that. Time was running out for the old house as the Corporation had decided to pull it down as part of their slum clearance operation.

We returned to Ballina the following week, totally broke, and stayed with Sarah's sister for a couple of days before moving into the dreadful flat. The important gig with Ruby Murray never materialised, so I had cut our honeymoon short for nothing. Now it was back to work as usual with the band.

~ Fifteen ~

Back in Ballina, I was playing five or six nights a week, and the extra money was much needed. Jack had given me a rise, insisting again that I keep my earnings a secret from the others.

He was slowly compromising on the showband question. Night after night as we played through the country, we were being told, 'Last night, such and such a band was here, and there was two thousand at the dance.'

Jack agreed to having the last part of the dances as showband: we could remove the chairs and music stands from the stage, and play rock and roll or any of the Top Twenty numbers that we could busk. I had bought a cheap guitar and learned three or four chords, and we formed our own skiffle group with washboard, bass and drums. We were knocking them dead with Lonnie Donegan numbers.

Meanwhile, conditions in our wretched flat were getting even worse. The roof leaked like a sieve. I can't remember where the loo was, or whether we had one at all — I do recall having to use a bucket at one stage. The flat was just one big, freezing cold room, and we couldn't warm it up. Everything smelled of damp — it was a horrible place. Eventually Sarah and I had to move. Her sister Kathleen offered us a room in her house and, although I was against the idea, I agreed to accept the offer for Sarah's sake. All this time, we were badgering the county council to provide us with somewhere decent to live, but the housing situation was so bad that no houses were being built in Ballina. We would have to wait until a house became vacant and hope that it would be offered to us.

Winter was setting in, and dancing was confined to

weekends, with an occasional midweek dance, usually in a large town — Cork, Limerick or Galway.

One night we were playing in the wilds of Mayo and were setting up the gear before the dance when the amplifier started to give trouble. Jack, who usually looked after the system, could get nothing out of it. A man came onto the stage and said, 'Give me a screwdriver and I'll take the back off. I know something about these things.'

He began to work on the amplifier, prodding about among the bare wires and connections, and then he said, 'Don't let anyone plug it in.'

Unfortunately, somebody thought he said, 'Plug it in', and put the plug into the mains socket. There was a crackling sound. The man gave a shriek and was thrown up into the air. Somebody told me later that there were sparks coming out of his trousers. He was thrown right off the stage, crashing down onto the dance-floor below.

People rushed to his assistance, but luckily he wasn't badly hurt — just shocked. We got the amplifier working at last, and after the dance we were having a cup of tea, and the same man was sitting at the table with us. Jack asked how he was.

'All right — I served my time as an electrician, so I've had a good few shocks in my time.'

'They say an electric shock is great for one's sex life,' I joked.

There was a dreadful silence, then Jack changed the subject and began to talk about fishing. Afterwards, when we got outside, Covey told me that the man was the local priest!

* * *

Early in December, Sarah was sick and stayed in bed for a day or two. I was concerned about her and sent for the doctor. On coming out of the bedroom, he grabbed my hand and shook it. 'You're going to be a father. You can expect young Bollard some time at the end of next August.'

Sarah is a very shy person. While I, like most men, was thrilled to hear that I was to be a father, Sarah didn't want anybody to know. I wanted to rush out into the market square and tell everybody, but I contented myself with writing and telling my mother. 'You didn't tell your mother, did you?' Sarah asked, when she saw the letter. I had to remind her that we were married!

Sarah was quite sick early in her pregnancy. We spent our first Christmas with Kathleen and her family, and again the band played at the North Mayo Hunt Ball. Again there was a bottle of brandy for the band which was left under the piano until the break, but this time there was one less to share it. Thank God my drinking problem was gone for good: during the previous year I'd had no craving or inclination to drink.

In Lent, the band embarked on another English tour, which was much the same as the previous year, playing in the same venues with the exception of Liverpool. This time we were using some of our showband material. Jack was now taking the tenor sax solos in the rock and roll numbers. On one memorable night in the Blarney Club in London, the girls dragged Covey off the stage — they loved him, and his up-tempo rock vocals and gyrations set the place alight. I used to think that if we only had a good guitar player, we could really rock. But Jack was convinced that the showband craze was doomed to failure. He had been well-known as a band-leader throughout Ireland for many years — he had too much to lose.

Naturally, I visited Liverpool although we didn't play there. All the family were delighted about the baby on the way, and of course Mum gave me things to bring home for Sarah.

* * *

Spring changed to summer, with the usual run of carnivals, marquees and ham and lettuce meals, while all the time showbands were springing up around the country. At one time there were thirty-seven in the city of Derry alone. They were really big in Northern Ireland, probably because of the influence of television. In Ballina we depended on Radio Luxembourg for our inspiration.

I bought myself a tape recorder that year — a Philips open-reel machine — and connected it to my radio to record the latest hits. The reception was pretty bad, constantly fading in and out, but I didn't care as long as I got the hits of the day. Covey and I would listen and learn and try them out with the lads in the band.

I realised that the dancers wanted to hear the songs played as near the original as possible, so instead of being vocalists, Covey and I had to become impressionists. Sometimes it worked; other times our efforts sounded pathetic.

On Sunday 6 September, we played in Collooney in Co. Sligo, and tried out a good few showband numbers. We were still excited and talking about it on the way home. The band-wagon dropped me off at Sarah's sister's house where we were still living, and I found that everyone was still up. I also found the midwife there — Sarah had gone into labour. She was three weeks overdue.

Sarah had a really tough time of it, being her first pregnancy, and the baby so big. She suffered dreadfully and I felt helpless. She had decided to have the baby at home as most women did at the time in that part of the country. The following afternoon, she gave birth to a ten-pound boy. She was exhausted, but the baby was fine and I was relieved and delighted. I agreed to call the baby Joseph as Sarah had prayed to St Joseph during her pregnancy, promising that if everything went well she would name the baby after him. So we had another Joseph in the family.

I remember my feelings well when I first held Joseph in my arms. Most babies cry all over their fathers; I cried all over my baby. What a big lad he is, I thought, and I think I said something moronic like, 'Another forward for Everton.' But inside I was thinking, 'Good Lord, I'm responsible for this new human being.' It was a bit daunting to know that I had someone else's life in my hands.

I ran into the other room and played the Paul Robeson hit, 'Mighty Like a Rose' on the piano, fairly bursting with pride. Holding your first child for the first time must be one of the greatest feelings in the world — even if you can't see him.

Joseph was a troublesome baby, seeming to spend most of his waking hours crying. Sarah had a dreadful time with him: I would often get home in the early hours of the morning and find her still awake and exhausted, trying to get him to sleep. I quickly learned how to change a nappy and make a bottle — and I didn't have to turn the light on while I did it.

* * *

After Christmas, Jack at last began to give serious thought to the Jack Ruane Orchestra becoming a showband. On returning from our English tour that spring, he finally relented. His son Jud, who by this time was an established trumpet player, also played guitar, and he was quite good. I started teaching the lads in the band the backing harmonies to Covey's rock numbers, the ooh-ahs and the bop-bops. I taught them by ear and they memorised what they'd been taught. Our first efforts were quite feeble, but we persevered and I even learnt to do the fancy steps on stage, movements we made as we sang. I had to learn verbally — 'two steps forward, one to the left and two back' — while at the same time singing harmony. I also played the piano standing up, Little Richard style, often throwing my leg up on the keyboard.

On one occasion, during a frenzied rock session, I ran the back of my thumb down the keyboard, Jerry Lee Lewis style. It caught in a key whose ivory covering was missing — there was blood everywhere, and my hand was in a mess for days.

* * *

At long last, the council in Ballina managed to find a house for Sarah, young Joseph and me. It was a lovely little house whose occupants had decided to go to England. It was in Mount Assumpta at the top of the town in a quiet area — we were thrilled. Here I was with a job I liked, a wife and son and a good house. What more could I ask for?

One thing that was bothering me was that Covey was drinking more and more. I could see that what had happened to me was happening to him. I tried to tell him where it would lead and that I'd been down the same road, but my words fell on deaf ears. Unlike me, he couldn't hide the fact that he was drunk, and would get abusive. I was really worried as I knew what an asset he was to the band and I wondered where it would all end.

~ Sixteen ~

The next eighteen months were really great. Sarah and Joseph were well, Joseph started walking and talking very early, the band was packing them in wherever we played. Then, on returning from our Lenten tour of England, Sarah told me that she was pregnant again. The baby would be born in December, just in time for Christmas.

A local lad from Ballina had joined us as a guitar player. Another local lad, Noel O'Neill, had been engaged mainly to sing country numbers and he had a terrific repertoire. I had begun to take an interest in country music too. Since I first heard George Jones being played in a café in Limerick, I have been a fan of country music, and George Jones is still one of my favourite country singers.

Phyllis had left the band, but she joined us on our English tours, which were now more frequent — we would travel over for a week or ten days, mainly to the north.

All this time, Covey's drinking was becoming worse. It came to a head one night when we were playing at the town hall in Ballina. There was a rumpus on stage between Jack and Covey. The following morning, Covey was gone and I never saw him again. After that, he went downhill, and some time later, I heard that he had died.

Of all the musicians in the band, I was closer to Covey than to anyone. He was a great fellow when he was sober, and we had many a laugh. I still feel that, in different circumstances, Michael O'Sullivan (Covey) could have been a big star.

* * *

Early in December, our second son, Noel, was born. Like Joseph, he was a big baby and it was a difficult birth. Noel was a quiet baby, sleeping soundly a lot of the time, unlike that cross little fellow, Joseph. With the family growing, I again had to persuade Jack to increase my wages.

About that time, Jack's young son, Jack junior, joined the band as bass guitar player. He wasn't anxious to join at first, but we urged him on, and he turned out to be one of the best bass guitar players I have ever heard.

In 1962, we had a gig in Ballyclare, Co. Antrim. We usually ended by playing the national anthem, but in Northern Ireland we never did this. On this occasion, Jack thanked everyone and was about to put his saxophone away when there was a shout from the hall, 'Play "God Save the Queen"!'

'We never play national anthems,' lied Jack.

'Well, you'll play one now.'

Jack knew 'God Save the Queen', and, having lived in England for so long, I knew it too, but the others didn't know it all.

'We never play national anthems,' Jack repeated, as others took up the shout in the hall.

'If you don't play "God Save the Queen", we'll fuck you and your fucking band wagon in the river.'

Jack hastily started to play the melody on the sax, I chimed in on the piano, the drummer, who hadn't a notion how it went, played it as an old-time waltz. I thought we'd be lynched. It was the strangest version of the British national anthem I have ever heard, but we got away with it.

* * *

In July 1962, the band set off on a tour of the Irish clubs in America. The preparations were vast — we must have practised every Irish song that was ever written. We drove to Shannon and flew to New York, where we played in the City Centre Irish Club for three consecutive nights. On each night there were two thousand people there. I remember singing 'The Old Bog Road' on the Saturday night, and hearing the people actually crying — women sobbing their hearts out.

Our guide, mentor and general dogsbody on the tour was

Joe Cahill, later to return to Ireland and make a name for himself in the cabaret scene as MC.

We travelled in a very large Chevrolet and Joe was our driver. I recall the morning we left New York for the long drive to Chicago. We were late and would have to hurry if we were to make the dance that night in Chicago. We were belting along at 105 m.p.h. when we heard the sound of a siren behind us. 'Jesus, the police,' Joe said, 'Leave the talking to me.'

Joe pulled in, and as the policeman came up to the car, he rolled down the window. 'Faith and begorra, Guard, and is it yourself that's in it? What might you be wanting me for?' he asked in the most overacted stage Irish I have ever heard.

'Where might you be going?' the policeman asked, with just a trace of an Irish accent.

'Sure, aren't we the Jack Ruane Showband from Ballina, in the lovely county of Mayo. We're going to play for our Irish emigrant friends in Chicago and, as the priest kept us late after Mass, giving us his blessing, we're behind time. Is that a Galway accent I detect?'

'It is indeed. I'm from Tuam in Co. Galway, and I often danced to your band back home. Listen, take it easy on the road, slow down a little. Is that blind lad still singing with ye? God, you'd stand in the snow to hear him sing "The Old Bog Road". Take it easy now. *Go n-éirí an bóthar leat.*'

* * *

We played in Chicago, Boston and the Catskill Mountains, and then went back to New York. We played only at weekends, so we had a lot of free time. During one of our free spells, Joe brought us to a dude ranch in Rothbury, Michigan for a three-day break. Known as the 'Jack and Jill Ranch', it was like a holiday camp. All the attendants were dressed as cowboys, and we slept in shacks.

The first night, one of the cowboys asked whether any of us wanted to go horse riding in the morning. I had never ridden a horse but said I'd give it a try. He was a bit apprehensive but promised to find a quiet horse for me.

Early next morning, after a typical cowboy breakfast of

baked beans, we made our way to the corral. I was given a hat and, dressed in my shorts, I was shown how to get up on the horse. I sat there rigid, bolt upright.

The rest of the gang had gone riding around the ranch, but they were afraid that, being blind, I might get hurt, so I had to plod around the corral with 'Buffalo Bill' leading the horse. I soon got tired of this and asked to be allowed to walk around alone. 'Where can I go after all? We're surrounded by the corral fence,' I reasoned.

He reluctantly unclipped the lead rein, and Champion the Wonder Horse — or maybe it was his brother — realised that he was free. At the same time, I remembered that if you wanted a horse to go, you kicked him in the belly. I did that, thinking he would just trot. I also decided to do my Lester Piggot impersonation, lying flat along his back.

He took off like the wind and bolted round and round the corral. After we'd been round about six times, with Buffalo Bill shouting at both of us, I felt the horse come up under me and we flew through the air over the corral fence, which was about three feet high. I landed with such a jolt in the saddle that I was sure Sarah need never again worry about getting pregnant. The pain was excruciating.

We took off down the track, in the direction the other horses had gone. I suppose he was used to going with them every day. I lay on his back, terrified, not knowing how to stop him. Afraid I'd fall off, I squeezed my knees together, which he took to be a sign to go faster. We hurtled along and all I could hear was the thud of his hoofs on the track. After a few minutes, I heard galloping behind, and Buffalo Bill caught up with us, came alongside and managed to slow Champion to a walk, then to a full stop.

We turned and walked slowly back to the corral, where I slid off in an ungainly manner, to the applause of everyone around. 'I thought you said you hadn't ridden before,' said Bill. 'You took the corral fence like a professional.'

'I didn't take it, Champion did. I hadn't any choice,' I explained as I went off to the John for some much needed relief.

* * *

When we returned from America, something happened which changed my life yet again. Before we left home, we had been playing five and six nights most weeks, and I was away from Sarah and the lads a great deal. Then we went to America for a month. I was really looking forward to being with them again as we drove home from Shannon, and I practically ran into the house. There were hugs and kisses, but I realised that something wasn't right. The boys were hesitant: they weren't quite sure who I was. How could they be, when I was so rarely home?

It was then the idea was born in me that, if I wanted to spend time with my family, I'd have to leave the band. I said nothing to Sarah at the time, but did a great deal of soul searching.

What could I do? I was a musician. I couldn't get work as a postman or a bus driver, or even as a road sweeper. But if I wanted to work as a musician, I was going to have to leave Ballina and move to Dublin.

I didn't care about the difficulties, I wanted to be with my boys as they grew up.

September saw us once again embark on an English tour. I knew it would be my last tour with the band. On the final night we played in Leeds. I was drinking coffee, alone with Jack. 'Jack, I've something to say to you.'

I think he expected me to ask for another rise in my wages.

'I'm leaving the band,' I told him. 'I'll stay until the Lenten tour, but I won't come on tour with you again. I want to spend more time with my family.'

He didn't answer for a long time. Then he said, 'If you just played three nights a week, would that help things, Joe?'

'It wouldn't work, Jack. I'm doing such a lot — vocals, keyboard, helping with the arrangements — it would be messy when I wasn't playing.'

I asked him to keep my departure to himself.

I could tell he was disappointed — he hardly spoke, all the way home to Ballina. 'What's wrong with the Head?' somebody asked. 'He should be over the moon, the tour was such a success. There's no pleasing some people.'

I didn't say a word.

Christmas came, and we were to play in Dublin on St Stephen's Day, and the following day in Dundalk. I suggested to Sarah that she and the boys might like to spend the Christmas season with her sister Mary in Dublin. 'You could stay for a week or two,' I said, knowing that I would try to keep her in Dublin until March, when I would join her.

Sarah was still unaware that I had given in my notice. While she and the boys were in Dublin, I was making frantic arrangements to get some of our furniture moved there. Mary had said that we could stay with her until we found a place of our own, but I had sworn her to secrecy about the move.

After two weeks, I rang Sarah from Portlaoise where we were playing, and suggested she might stay another two weeks, as she was really enjoying herself and so were the lads. Then, three weeks later, when I had made all the necessary arrangements, I rang her from Athlone, where we were playing for a big dance. I asked whether she was enjoying herself and, when she said that she was, I told her how I'd given notice in September.

'I didn't tell you, as I wanted to make it easy for you to leave Ballina,' I explained. 'We'll stay in Dublin with Mary for a while — ask her to tell you about it.' I was amazed how calmly she took the news.

In Ballina, when the word got out, people were amazed. 'Joe Bollard leaving Jack Ruane? It couldn't happen.'

Coincidentally, my last gig with the band was in the same venue as my first, the town hall in Ballina. The hall was thronged — Jack was about to go to England for his Lenten tour. During the dance, he tried once more to get me to change my mind, even offering me more money, but I was adamant. Travelling with a showband was all right for a single man, but it wasn't for me, now that I had commitments.

Tears were shed after the dance, and the following morning, I headed for Dublin, along with our drummer, Dessie, who was going home to Arklow for a few days.

I had spent seven years in Ballina, most of them happy. I remember wondering as the train pulled out, where those three guys were who had been discussing me the night of my second gig with the band. I had shown them what I could do: I had worked hard, played hard, kept pace with everyone. I had never been a passenger at any time and never allowed my blindness to be used to further my career.

I was moving away from Ballina and a part of my life which I will never forget. It would be many years before I would return.

~ Seventeen ~

Settling down in Dublin was a complete culture shock for four-year-old Joseph and Noel who was two. Sarah and I had lived in a city before, but they had come from a quiet west of Ireland town, to the heart of Dublin. They found it overwhelming.

We moved in with Sarah's sister Mary, who had two boys of her own. We had our own bedroom, and shared the rest of the house. It was cramped, but we didn't mean to be there for long and the sisters got on well together. The boys had a great time. Joseph was fascinated by the double-decker buses, little knowing that one day he would be a bus driver. Noel had a passion for shopping in the big stores and would cry when he had to come out. We took them to the zoo, the cinema and, on St Patrick's Day, to O'Connell Street to see the parade. I thought Noel would burst with excitement as he sat on my shoulders, watching everything.

As for me, one of the first things I did was to go to the headquarters of the Irish Federation of Musicians — our union — and let them know that I was available for any work that might come in.

In those days, weddings usually took place in the morning after eleven o'clock Mass, with the reception starting at around one. There wouldn't be a band playing — a piano player was the norm. The guests danced to the piano and sang their party pieces. Everyone had to be out of the hotel by half past five.

My first wedding gig was at the Clontarf Castle Hotel, where I played for three long hours. Luckily, the piano was a good one and the guests seemed to like what I did. The owner of the hotel, Eddy Regan, happened to be there, was impressed, and offered me more work. I got a lot of wedding work from him after that. In those days, the Clontarf Castle wasn't the big cabaret venue it is today.

I contacted many hotels in Dublin, saying that I was available for wedding receptions, and the work kept coming in. I confess, I hated playing at some of these receptions — making people enjoy themselves while often the piano was simply dreadful, with half the keys not working and the rest horribly out of tune. But I got on with it and tried my best.

There was one reception which I will never forget. It took place in a large, popular hotel, noted for its weddings. As I started to play the piano, I noticed that there was a tense atmosphere in the room. I mentioned it to one of the lounge waiters when he brought me a cup of coffee.

'You're dead right,' he said. 'The two families can't stand each other — talk about Romeo and Juliet. If there's a row, get under the piano!'

Everything went smoothly as I went through my usual routine of getting the guests up to dance and sing. Then I announced a short break while the bride changed into her going-away outfit, normally a matter of about ten minutes. We waited. Ten minutes ... fifteen ... twenty.... People were getting restless. 'What's keeping her?' 'Where the hell is she?' 'It can't take her that long to change.'

'I'll go and see what's keeping her,' said the bridegroom. Two minutes later, there was an almighty yell from the top of the stairs, and people started to run. The bridegroom had found the bride and the best man naked on the bed, having their own little honeymoon. They had been engaged to each other at one time and were renewing acquaintances.

The father and mother of all rows broke out: chairs, tables and bar stools flew; there were screams and shouts; the best man was flung down the stairs naked; while the bridegroom's mother dragged her new daughter-in-law along the corridor by the hair. The staff tried to intervene but the guards had to be called.

I sat as instructed under the piano, and was joined by some of the bar staff who gave me a running commentary. It took three-quarters of an hour to clear the place, and there were ambulances and squad cars outside.

I made up my mind to stop playing at wedding receptions as soon as I could afford to do so. I was tired of making people sing who didn't want to sing, for people who didn't want to hear them.

For a few months, I found myself doing many strange gigs and in some unusual venues. My showband training stood to me, bringing out my ability to improvise, impersonate, fit in anywhere and adapt. For some months, I even played bass guitar in a céilí band. I also sang at wedding Masses, little realising how much of that kind of work I would be doing later on in my life.

The Mass was in Latin at that time, so you could sing practically all through the ceremony. I didn't play the organ then — I just sang. I went to Walton's and bought sheet music of Gounod's 'Ave Maria', César Franck's 'Panis Angelicus' and 'Just for Today'. I had to learn to sing without a microphone and to project my voice down through the whole church.

Then in June, I heard that The Silver Tassie, a pub in Loughlinstown, Co. Dublin, had advertised for a piano player for the lounge. I phoned the manager and arranged an interview.

* * *

At that time, The Silver Tassie was owned by a Scotsman, Alex Pinkerton. It was the regular haunt of the hundreds of Scottish tourists who used to flock to Bray, about four miles away, for their holidays. This was at a time when Bray used to be crammed with visitors in the summer. All the hotels and B&Bs were full to capacity. There was the Glasgow fortnight and the Northern Ireland fortnight. English, Scottish and Welsh holidaymakers thronged the sea front by day and the pubs at night. The launch of the car ferry encouraged tourists to bring their cars with them, though, and they began to bypass Bray as they headed for other parts of Ireland. This marked the end of Bray as the holiday centre it used to be.

Shortly before my interview for The Silver Tassie, I had a brainwave. I remembered on my last English tour with the band visiting a club in Leeds where a musician was playing an electronic organ. I was fascinated and had a long chat with the

~ Eighteen ~

Our flat in Bray was the top of three in a very old house. It was by far the best of the three, having a sitting room, bathroom, kitchen and two large bedrooms, one of which we used as a playroom for the boys. The owner lived in England, so we had to pay our rent each week at the auctioneer's office in town. The rent was quite high, but at least we had our own place at last, and I had my job and a regular income.

The day we moved in, a force nine gale was howling, rain lashed the huge windows of the flat, and we could hear the sea crashing against the promenade at the bottom of the road. Sarah was not too enamoured with it but the boys were really excited. They had been restricted in space in Dublin, but now they had a big playroom, and a wide staircase to run up and down — they were thrilled.

We were living in a pleasant part of the town, with a school opposite us and the church at the top of the road. The town centre was only ten minutes' walk away, and the sea front five minutes' walk, at the end of the road. A bus stop opposite the gate made it really convenient for me to get to work. Each evening, Sarah would put me on the bus, and one of the staff from The Silver Tassie would meet me at the end of my journey. On the return journey, the bus conductor would help me off the bus and take me to my gate. At the time, mobility was quite a problem for me. I couldn't manage a white cane, so I didn't use one, but depended on other people to get me around.

The work was fantastic. The Silver Tassie was then the only establishment providing live entertainment in the area. I was playing everything from Beethoven to The Beatles. Many top musicians came to hear what I was doing, with a view to starting something similar in their own areas. It was a complete change from showband work as I was on my own musically, responsible for everything I was doing.

I played requests, and was often amused by the attempts people made at some of the titles — especially if it was a guy trying to impress his girlfriend. 'Can you play Handel's "Lager"?' 'Do you know Beethoven's "Roll Over"?' 'Can you play "Madame Butterfly"?' 'Could you play "The Blue Daniel", please?' One of the best was when a man with a Cork accent asked for the 'Have a Banana' from *Carmen*.

* * *

The move to Bray was a success, although Sarah took some time to settle down. There is an old saying, 'A new house means a new baby', and so it was with us. Our third son, Declan, was born in hospital in December 1965. He was a very active little fellow and, according to the nurse, exactly like me.

Joseph had started school at Presentation College, almost immediately opposite our flat. I can't really compare Joseph's first day at school with my own. He came home at one o'clock, while I didn't come home until Christmas. He was delighted to be going, although he was only four; we were rather sad. Joseph loves a challenge, but Noel is different. We didn't send the younger boys to school until they were five. Noel was a quiet child who hero-worshipped Joseph.

The boys' First Communion days were in contrast to mine too. For one thing, there were fifty or sixty boys taking part, so it was much more of an occasion. I played the organ for both days, and later on for Declan, the youngest, and it helped me to feel that I was part of their Communion.

Joseph and Noel loved their new home. We were a close family, spending a lot of time together. During the summer we would take a picnic and climb Bray Head, staying there until late in the evening, or we would take the train to Greystones for the day. In bad weather, we would play games at home in the big playroom, even cricket and football. I was enjoying being with the boys immensely. This was what I had left the band for, and my night job left me free to be with them most days.

One day, we were all playing football in the college field opposite the apartment. I was listening to the ball bouncing along, using my keen hearing to tell me when it was coming my way. I'd had plenty of practice at school in Liverpool.

As we played, I heard a man's voice say, 'Aren't you Joe Bollard, the blind organist who plays in The Silver Tassie?'

'That's right,' I replied. The others told me afterwards that his mouth just dropped open.

'But — has there been a miracle? Can you see again?'

'No. I'm still blind.'

'But you're kicking a football. I've been watching you. You're very good. How do you do it?'

'I just listen hard and when the ball comes near me, I have a go. I can hear it bounce and I can hear it roll through the grass. I know where the goalposts are because Joseph is in goal and he calls to me when I have the ball so I can get my direction. My family don't make any allowances for my blindness — they tackle me the same as anyone else.'

'Do you mind if I go home and get my camera?'

I said I didn't mind, but I wondered what all the fuss was about when he came back shortly afterwards and started snapping here and snapping there.

A few days later, there was a picture in the local paper, showing our game, with the usual corny headline about the brave man who overcomes his affliction and plays football with his family. I didn't consider myself 'brave'. When the customers at The Silver Tassie congratulated me, I said, as so often before and since, 'It's only my eyes that don't work.'

* * *

About three months after our arrival in Bray, I was playing in The Silver Tassie when a quiet-spoken man asked me to play something for him. When I'd finished, he asked me where I lived. 'You're in our parish,' he said, 'Queen of Peace. I'm the curate there. Do you ever play the organ in church?'

'Not since I was at school,' I said.

'Sometimes our organist isn't available to play. Would you perhaps be able to help us out?'

I don't consider myself a religious person, but I go to Mass on Sunday, say the odd prayer during the day and have a good repertoire of hymns, thanks to the nuns who taught me. I agreed to help if I could.

The following weekend I was coming out of Mass with the boys when a hand was placed on my shoulder. 'I'm Father Breen. I was talking to you in The Silver Tassie during the week and you said you might be able to help us out. Well, our organist can't do the Miraculous Medal devotions tomorrow night — can you play for us? I'll drive you down to The Silver Tassie afterwards so you won't be late for work.'

On Monday evening, Fr Breen called for me and, as I climbed the gallery steps to the organ, I thought, what am I letting myself in for? I'm definitely not doing this on a regular basis. How wrong can you be? Since that summer evening thirty-two years ago, I've been involved in 90 per cent of the music in our parish. As well as playing for Masses and other church ceremonies, I formed a choir at the end of 1965, and have trained and arranged music for it ever since. I play and sing for weddings and funerals, Holy Week ceremonies, Christmas celebrations. Recently, I was awarded a medal from the Pope for my musical contribution to the parish of Our Lady, Queen of Peace.

When I started playing there, the 'organ' was just an old asthmatic harmonium, which had to be pedalled up and down to produce any sound. The rope connecting the pedals to the bellows kept breaking, and people were often shaken out of their prayerful trance by a crash from the gallery as the pedal broke. I was asked to play there more and more often, and towards the end of the year, the organist left altogether and I took over officially.

* * *

At that time, my work at the church was voluntary, but the word spread about my playing and singing, and I began to get a lot of paid work for weddings. The showband era in Ireland was over and the ballad era had taken its place. The Clancy Brothers were popular, and every pub echoed to the sound of ballads. At The Silver Tassie, the music was quieter. One person described it as 'more sedate', which I daresay it was, although I wasn't sure that I liked my music being described as sedate.

Although I was working five nights a week, money was a constant worry. Our flat was expensive and I couldn't rely on getting enough wedding work to keep the family. We were sending the boys to the Presentation College, and their school fees had to be met.

Then one night, Alex Pinkerton came down to the lounge where I was playing and told me that he and his wife had decided to retire to Spain. The pub had been sold.

'One of two things will happen,' said Alex. 'Either the new owner, Mr Fitzsimon, will keep you on or, if he doesn't want to have music, he will make you a present of the organ, so that you can get work elsewhere.'

Mr Fitzsimon liked my playing and decided to keep me on, which pleased me. I worked for him for about two and a half years. It turned out that he didn't want just me in the corner, playing seductive music, singing romantic songs — he wanted a bit of sing-along music to liven the place up at the weekends.

I carried on until 1969, when I heard rumours that The Silver Tassie was to be sold again. Mr Fitzsimon, an easygoing man, was praising me one night as I was packing up: 'Another great night, Joe, fabulous night —'

'Look,' I said. 'There's a rumour that this place is for sale.'

'Yes, it's on the market, but only to see what it's worth, what we might expect to get for it.'

Within a month, the place had been sold, and the new owner didn't want music. Although I was losing my job, I expected the earlier arrangement to stand, whereby I was to keep the organ. It was in good condition, so I didn't foresee too many difficulties in getting work in Bray.

There was a big celebration, and the last night in The Silver Tassie was fantastic. However, I was out of work, at least for the time being.

Some time before this, the woman who owned our flat had come home from England and asked us to move out of our spacious top-floor flat into the basement flat. We had already applied to Bray County Council for a house, and we agreed to move into the damp basement, because we thought that the council would be obliged to give us a house.

Our living conditions were awful.

* * *

When I went down to The Silver Tassie to see about the organ, the new owner told me that he had bought the place lock, stock and barrel, including all the furniture — and the organ.

The original agreement had been with Alex Pinkerton. The subsequent owners were not obliged to keep to it.

At that time, the main cabaret venue in Bray was the International Hotel, which was burned down some years later. There was a big cabaret room, and it was one of the most popular around. Busloads of people would come to it from Dublin. Not long after I left The Silver Tassie, there was a big charity night at the International, and I was asked to sing. The MC was Ernie Pigott — a wonderful singer, and a very good man at his job. He sang and led the group. There was a 'Cordovox' (electronic accordion) player, a drummer and Ernie.

I went in and performed four of five numbers. Afterwards, when we were talking in the band room, Ernie and I discovered that we had a lot in common, music-wise. Suddenly he turned to me, and said, 'Look, Joe, I'm not happy here. I want to leave. Can I come and see you about an idea I've got, at your home?'

The following afternoon, he put his idea to me. I was playing a keyboard at that time. 'After hearing you singing and playing,' said Ernie, 'I want to suggest to you that we form a group of our own. We could get a drummer; you can play keyboards; we can have a little trio and do the cabaret scene.'

I was out of work — what had I to lose? Ernie was to find the work, do the bookings, and we would split the money down the middle.

We picked up a drummer named Vinnie Keane, and also a guitar player named Jay Malone. Ernie organised a number of gigs for us. We didn't do any rehearsals — I had a piano at home and we would run over a couple of songs, and that was that. We hit it off from day one.

Ernie got us five nights' work a week. We worked in the Cliff Castle Hotel in Dalkey, which is no longer in existence, and also in a place called the Noggin Inn, a huge cabaret place. It was the early 1970s and the cabaret scene was very popular.

Around the same time, the Urban District Council contacted me and said they'd found a house for us in Wolfe Tone Square. It was in a dreadful condition, and had no electricity — there was still gas light. It was painted a dreary green. An old lady had lived there on her own.

We moved in without too much fuss, and got lots of help from our neighbours. We had to get electricity put in and all sorts of essentials, so we were broke by the time we moved in. But we didn't mind — we had decided it was where we would stay.

* * *

The Ernie Pigott Group, as it was called, really took off. Soon we were playing six nights a week. Jay, the guitar player, sang; I sang; the drummer was brilliant.

This continued for about eighteen months, and Ernie and I were great friends. Even on our days off, we would meet and talk. If my blindness was a problem for him, he never said.

~ Nineteen ~

In 1974, I decided that the time had come to do something about my mobility — or the lack of it. As the boys grew up they used to come everywhere with me, especially Joseph, the eldest. If I wanted to go to the shops, they brought me there, and they brought me to visit friends. I was doing a lot of wedding work on Saturday mornings, and Joseph would always come with his dad.

Noel would come along too sometimes, and I tried to make it a bit of an adventure for them. They always got well rewarded with sweets and goodies. However, as Joseph was getting to the age of playing on the rugby or soccer team for his school, I began to feel that quite often he would rather be with his friends. Sarah couldn't come because Declan was still quite young, and anyway I didn't want to make a family occasion of it, by arriving with my wife and children.

What with the wedding work and the fact that I was playing with the group five nights a week, I just had to make up my mind to do something about my mobility problem.

I had a friend, Anne Hely, with whom I'd been at school for many years. She had married in Ireland and come to live in Tralee. I knew that she had a guide dog, but I had always looked on guide dogs as circus performers — who would put their faith in a dog? I wrote to Anne, asking her advice, and about a week later, she arrived with her dog. She stayed in a local hotel, and came to visit, bringing her young son with her.

After about a quarter of an hour, Anne said to Sarah, 'I want to go and get some cigarettes. Where's the shop?'

'Hang on a minute,' said Sarah, 'One of the youngsters will run and get them for you.'

'No, they needn't do that.' Anne put on her coat, asking, 'Do you want anything from the shop?'

Then she put the harness she'd just shown me on her dog, went out the door, across the road, and the 300 yards or so to the corner shop. She got what she went to get and came back.

This astounded me because all she had asked Sarah was, 'Where's the shop?' I had lived in the house for years and had never ventured that far on my own, even with a cane. Anne had been in the house for fifteen minutes, had gone off with her dog, got what she wanted and come back.

We sat and talked about guide dogs and Anne answered every question I asked her.

'There's a guide-dog convention being held in Co. Cork in six or eight weeks' time,' she told me. 'Why don't you come down, as all the guide-dog owners get together and you can ask questions to your heart's content. A Mrs Mary Dunlop is organising it, and it's on from Friday until Sunday lunch-time.'

I promised to think about it.

Anne went off home to Tralee after a few days, but she kept in contact, telling me all sorts of things about guide dogs. I was almost convinced.

I couldn't go to Cork for a whole weekend, because I was working on Saturday and Sunday night with the group, but I headed off on the Friday on my own. Somebody put me on the train and there were two guide-dog owners travelling, so we talked about the dogs. There weren't many in Ireland at the time. We arrived at the convention, where one of the speakers was John Weekes, who was head of the Guide Dogs for the Blind Association in Britain. There was no association in Ireland then. I had already learned that if I wanted to go for training with a dog, I'd have to go to Exeter in Devonshire.

I stayed overnight, and listened and learned. On the Saturday, I set off on my own. I got a taxi to the station in Cork, was put on a train, was taken off in Dublin and put in another taxi, which took me to a bus, which went to Bray. Somebody met me there, and I remember feeling that I was being passed from Billy to Jack — if I had a guide dog, I could do it all on my own.

I had more or less decided to go for a dog, although at the time Sarah wasn't happy about it. She didn't think that a dog would be all that useful to me, and, naturally enough, she was worried in the beginning — as I was. Now, however, she is one of the biggest champions of guide dogs that you could find.

* * *

Having written to Exeter, to enquire about applying for a guide dog, I heard nothing for a couple of months. Then I got a letter, a form to fill in, and had a medical check-up. Another two months passed before a trainer came from Exeter, to visit me and to meet other Irish applicants.

When he arrived, the trainer, Paul, brought a harness and a lead. He had come mainly to see my house and the environment I lived in. After lunch, we filled out all necessary information about my life and my work. Then Paul said, 'Now we're going out around your neighbourhood for a walk.'

'What for?' I asked.

'I want to judge the speed you walk at, so we can get a dog that walks at your speed naturally. Then I want to judge the tension of your left arm, which will be holding the harness.'

'What's the idea of that?'

'I want to see whether you grip the harness tightly or if you are relaxed,' said Paul. 'Each guide-dog owner is different. I'm going to pretend to be a dog and you must give me orders as if I were a dog.'

'Oh.' I felt rather stupid about this and reluctant to do it, but I unwillingly did as I was told.

Outside my gate, Paul began to 'be the dog'. I held the harness in my hand, holding it loosely as he had told me to do. Paul was on my left-hand side, standing still.

'Tell me to go forward,' he said. 'Give me the instruction, "Forward", and speak as if you were giving orders to a dog.'

We had already aroused a lot of curiosity among the local children playing in the street. A crowd of them gathered round as I said firmly, 'Forward!', and we started to walk.

When we reached the edge of the pavement, Paul, being the dog, stopped, and I had to give him instructions to step down. We walked along and I gave all the instructions I had been told. Then a young lad ran up to us and said, 'Hey, Mr Bollard, do you know there's no dog on the end of that? — There's a man.'

We were being followed like the Pied Piper by herds of children as we went down our street, and I felt *so stupid*. Then we arrived at the pedestrian crossing and Paul said, 'Tell me to sit.' This is necessary in the early stages of training, but not once you've got used to a dog.

'If I tell you to sit and you sit, I'm walking away and leaving you here,' I said. By this time twenty or thirty people, grown-ups as well as children, were following Mr Bollard and his 'dog'. I had seldom felt so embarrassed or so foolish. However, when we got back, Paul said that he said was very pleased.

About two weeks later, I got a letter from the Guide Dogs for the Blind Association, telling me that I had been accepted for a dog, and that they would let me know when one was available. It was about ten months later that I heard that there was a dog for me.

* * *

In the meantime, I had finished playing with the group. Ernie and I had had a difference of opinion. We had agreed when I joined the group that we could work separately if we wished, but only on nights when the group wasn't working. One evening I went to a wedding as a guest — it was the daughter of a dear friend of mine who was getting married.

The group was working, and I had great difficulty in getting a 'dep', as we called it, to fill in for me. Everybody I rang was busy. In the end, for the first and last time in my life, I recommended someone I had never heard.

Of course, at the wedding I was asked to sing and, although I protested that it was my day off, I got up and sang a couple of songs, just as a guest.

When I got home, Sarah told me that Jay Malone, the guitar player, had phoned, and that the keyboard player I had recommended was absolutely dreadful. There were going to be problems.

The following evening, the group was playing at our regular venue, the Cliff Castle Hotel in Dalkey. I was assembling the keyboard, kneeling on the floor, when Ernie knelt down beside me and suddenly let fly. He said that I had let him down to do another gig; that someone had seen me up on stage singing;

and that the guy I had recommended was vile, and couldn't play to save his life. I tried to have it out with Ernie during the interval, but he just got more and more angry. Finally he said, 'You'd never have got anywhere in the music game if you didn't use your blindness to get work.'

I rarely get angry, but his remark hit a raw nerve.

'If that's what you think,' I said, 'I'm resigning from the group.' I was so furious that for some time I couldn't go back on stage. When I did, I couldn't concentrate. Ernie had accused me of something I had never done in my life, something that I would frown on any other blind person for doing.

Two days later, we met for another gig and my anger had simmered down, although I was still annoyed. I said that I would stay on only if Ernie apologised. He refused, only repeating his point, although Jay and Vinnie both disagreed with him. The group broke up.

It's only fair to say that at that time Ernie had domestic problems and a major drink problem. He may have been looking for a way out of the group. What a pity, if that was the case, that he should do it in that way. I had seen him as a real friend.

We met twice or three times in the next twenty years, and we were polite when we met. He has since gone to his reward.

* * *

The letter from Exeter asked whether I could attend a guide-dog training course for a month.

There were four other blind Irish people travelling to Exeter — three men and one woman — and we were to fly there from Dublin, to start on 30 June. We paid our own fares, but our board and lodging at the guide-dog centre — which was first class — cost a nominal amount of about £5 a week.

This was the first time since the American trip with the Jack Ruane Band that I had been away from home for so long, and Sarah was very upset when the letter came from the association. She still felt sceptical about me and guide dogs.

The other four Irish trainees and I met at the airport. There were two from the country and three from Dublin, and we were all anxious. There was a service between Dublin and Exeter then, so we arrived at Exeter and were met by three trainers.

In those days, the groups of trainees consisted of twelve in a class with three trainers. In Ireland now, there are just four in a class, and in England six or eight.

On meeting our trainers, the first thing that struck me was their formal address: 'Hello, Mr Bollard, I'm your trainer.'

'Hello,' I said. 'Cut out the Mr Bollard — I'm Joe.'

He didn't answer and we got into a van.

We arrived at the centre, where the trainer showed us our rooms — two of us to a room. He called us Mr Bollard, Mr O'Reilly, Mr Loughran — it seemed strange to us. Later, it was explained to us that they maintained that it encouraged the student/teacher relationship, and that if we were on first-name terms, we wouldn't pay as much attention to the teacher. I thought this policy ridiculous, and it has since been dropped.

When we assembled, we met the other eight people in the class. They were mainly from the south of England, as Exeter then covered the south. There are many other centres now. We were all very nervous — none of us had applied for a dog before.

After tea, I expected to be given my dog. But instead there was a sort of get-together, and we were introduced to the trainers. My trainer wasn't Paul who had visited me in Ireland, but a man called Andy. After some general discussion, we were asked, 'Any questions?'

'Yes.' I said. 'Where's my dog?'

I learned that we might not get our dogs for three days.

As I lay in bed that night, listening to the sounds around me, a few dogs barking, a train somewhere off in the distance, the guy in the other bed snoring, I was reminded of my first night in Ballina, all those years before. I remembered how I'd been determined to succeed but felt ever so lonely. It was the same now. All my life I've had spells of feeling like that.

The next morning, we started our lectures and were told the legal end of things. I realised that I was with a great crowd of people — they must have been apprehensive as I was, but the jokes were flying, and I settled in quickly. I found myself working as interpreter for some of my Irish friends from the country. One was from Longford, another from Tipperary, and they had local accents.

After the lecture, we were shown the equipment we would

be using — the harness, the lead, the whistle. Then they did what I had already done with Paul: we went out, each with a trainer acting as a dog — one man and his man, I joked. We learned about the special footwork required when coming up to pavements and so on. I still felt hesitant and unsure.

We had arrived on a Saturday, and on the Tuesday we were told we were going to get our dogs.

'We want you to go up to your room and sit on the floor,' said Andy. 'Your dog will be brought to your room, put in through the door and left with you. You must make a fuss of him, sitting on the floor so as to be less frightening for him. Later on, we'll give you a lead and you can bring him downstairs.'

Then each of us was told about the dog we were getting. Andy came around to me and said, 'Your dog is a Labrador and his name is Ian.'

'What a name for a dog,' I thought.

I went up to my room and sat on the floor, while Pat Reilly, who was sharing my room, went into a different room. I heard a scraping of paws on the lino, and the next moment Andy popped the dog into the room, closed the door and went away.

The dog stood inside the door and whimpered. I called him but he didn't move, and started to whinge and cry for the trainer. Eventually, he came over to me, sniffed at me and bounded back to the door where he yelped to get out.

'Hey,' I said. 'You and I are going to spend the next few years together so you'd better get used to me and, what's more, you'd better get to like me.'

I began to worry, but I kept talking to him, and at last he came to me. I gave him big hugs and eventually he licked my face, but he was still listening for his trainer.

Andy popped the lead into the room and Ian made a dive for the door as soon as the lead was on. When we'd got ourselves downstairs, he saw Andy and made a dive for him. We were in a big room called the students' lounge, and we sat down with our dogs lying beside us.

The dogs were excited, and when guide dogs get excited, they have a habit of breaking wind. I think that this is especially a problem with guide dogs because of their high-protein soya-based diet. With twelve dogs in the room, all breaking wind, I said to the guy sitting beside me, 'Don't light a cigarette or we'll all be blown to kingdom come.'

We were told that this would wear off when the dogs got used to us, but it didn't wear off for Ian and, at the most awkward times, he would break wind, and it really was pungent.

When we went to bed that night, there was a bed for the dogs in the room I shared with Pat. We were both tired out, but the dogs wanted to play and were rolling about having great fun and keeping us awake. We had no idea what to do about it. At last the trainer, who slept next door, shouted, 'What's that noise?'

'The dogs want to play.'

'Well, you don't want them to play, do you? Take control of your dogs — tell them to be quiet.'

'On your bed, get into your bed,' I commanded — and the dog did it. That was the first instruction I had given to a guide dog, and he had obeyed me.

* * *

I became friendly with a guy called Pete, originally from Northern Ireland, who had lived in England, been in the RAF and had lost his sight. Our dogs were brothers, Ian and Ilk. Our friendship lasted for many years, but sadly, Pete died not so long ago. He had had a hard life and all sorts of problems apart from his eyesight. He told me where he carried tablets in case he should fall asleep or zonk out: 'These tablets here, in this shaped box, stick one into my mouth and get medical help.'

Pete didn't take anything too seriously, except his guide-dog training. Everything else was just a joke and we sometimes just fell on the floor laughing.

When we had had our dogs for two days, we went for our first walk. We and the dogs were all put in the back of a big van, and we headed off for a street in Exeter. By this time, we had learnt how to put the harness on our dogs properly. I had put the harness on Ian and was standing beside him, and Andy told me, 'Tell your dog to go f-o-r-w-a-r-d.' He spelt it so that the dog wouldn't move.

I opened my mouth to speak, and all of a sudden, I froze, and my heart started to beat rapidly. It was a roasting hot day, I remember, and I just couldn't move.

This was unfamiliar territory. All sorts of things ran through my mind. What happens if the dog sees a cat? What happens if it sees a train? What happens if it crosses the road? I had come all this way, been to all this trouble to get a dog to increase my mobility, and now I found I had no faith in the dog.

Yes, I had played football. I had played in the street, but this was different. There was nobody ahead of me to direct me, nobody to shout, 'This way, Joe!' The open ground ahead was alien territory and I just couldn't trust Ian. In the same way, I had had no trust in myself when I learned to use the white cane. I had always been useless with the cane.

Andy kept saying, 'Come on, Mr Bollard, can you hear me?' but I still froze. The sweat began to pour down the back of my neck and I could feel it. I was soaking and I was shaking.

'Come on,' Andy said.

'I can't,' I said. 'I can't move.'

So Andy told me to sit down, take it easy for a while, and take three or four deep breaths.

All the others had gone and I felt ridiculous. I lined myself up with the dog again and said in a timid voice, 'Forward.'

The dog didn't move.

'Don't speak to your dog like that,' said Andy. 'Put some emphasis on the word.'

I took another deep breath. 'Forward!'

The dog began to walk. I began to move and my feet felt like lead — it was sheer terror. We had to walk a hundred yards, and I made it eventually. We got into the van and went home.

During dinner, Pete said, 'What's the matter, Head? You're usually full of jokes.'

'It's not going to work, Pete,' I said. I was nearly in tears.

'Why?' he asked.

'I can't do it. I'm terrified.'

That evening, I had a talk with Andy. 'Look,' he said; 'that happens to lots of new guide-dog owners. But we never thought it would happen to you. We thought you'd fly through it. It'll be different tomorrow, you'll see.'

But it wasn't.

The next day, we went for a longer walk, and I still couldn't do it. I was really upset, and that evening, I went to see the head man, John Weekes, whom I'd met at the convention.

'I've made a decision,' I said to him. 'I want to go home. Guide dogs are not for me. It's not working.'

'How many walks have you had?' he asked.

'Two, and they've both been disastrous.'

He told me that if I felt the same way at the same time the following week, they would send me home. 'You're here for a month, but give it a week,' he said.

I agreed reluctantly, and later we went to a folk club, leaving the dogs behind, and had one hell of an evening's fun. I sang a few Irish folk songs, Pete sang too. I think that broke the ice.

I slept like a top that night, and the next day we did up kerbs and down kerbs with the dogs, which was difficult but I began to feel that it wasn't quite so bad. It got easier and easier as the week passed, and when the week was up, I was able to tell John Weekes, 'Yes, I'll stay with it, I'll give it a whirl.'

~ Twenty ~

At the Centre, Ian and I were hitting it off, and the training progressed smoothly. It was great to ring home and say that I was getting on with Ian, although I think the boys were disappointed that I hadn't got a German Shepherd.

Pete was generally up to something, and he and I got into a few scrapes. One day, we went on a long walk and, when we got out of the van, one of the ladies got out behind us. While she was getting into line, Pete put his dog on her harness.

So she was saying, 'Forward, Forward,' and the dog was taking no notice. She called Paul, one of the trainers, and said, 'What's the matter with my dog? It won't go.'

'That's hardly surprising, Mrs Meagher,' he said. 'It isn't your dog.'

There was a great rivalry between Pete and me — 'My dog's better than your dog' and that sort of thing. In fact, the two dogs, being brothers, were much alike and knew one another very well.

One day we were 'doing traffic lights', which meant walking up to the lights and getting help crossing the road. The idea was to wait at the traffic lights at a very busy crossing, and when you felt or heard someone beside you, you would say, 'Excuse me, could you give me a hand across the road?'

Pete was a great man for the women. In the van, he was saying, 'I'm going to get the greatest bit of crumpet to take me across — a real sexy bird — wait till you see.'

Pete was about twenty yards in front of me and I heard him telling his dog, 'Find the kerb, find the kerb.' I was standing, waiting for my turn, and I heard him ask for a hand across the road. A nice genteel voice said, 'Yes sir, certainly sir,' and he was chattering with her all the way across. When he reached the far side, he shouted to me, 'There you are, Bollard! What about that for a nice piece of crumpet? Now let's see what you can do.'

'Go on, Ian, find the kerb,' I said.

The next minute I felt a presence beside me, and politely asked for a hand across the road. This dear old lady who must have been eighty said in a broad accent, 'Yes my dear, I'll give you an 'and across. I'll put my shopping down 'ere.' She hobbled across the road and then she patted me on the shoulder. 'Now aren't you a very brave boy.'

Pete was in bits laughing. 'How about that for your bit of crumpet then, Bollard?' he joked.

In the evenings, there was no training, and we sat in the students' lounge. One evening when I went into the lounge, there were three students there — one from England, and two from Ireland — all totally blind, with their dogs. The van had been left outside the door and I had discovered that it was unlocked. There was one trainer who had a habit of jingling the loose change in his pocket, so we always knew when he was around. I was very good at imitating this trainer's accent, and I went into the lounge, rattling the change in my pockets, and said, in this guy's accent, 'Okay, you lot, this evening we're going to have extra training. I want you all to go out and sit in the van. I'm going to collect the others and I may be a few minutes, but just take your dogs, get in the van and wait for me.'

They all took their dogs, went out and got into the van. And they sat in the van ... and sat in the van.... After half an hour, the real trainer found them there and asked what they were doing. 'You sent us out here yourself,' they said.

'*I* did?' He was totally astounded.

He asked me what they were doing there and I pleaded ignorance, but I think he suspected me all the same.

Another time, I needed to get even with Pete, who'd played some joke or other on me. There were kennel maids there, and they were always full of fun. I asked one of them if she could lend me a pair of her knickers. She knew I was up to some sort of joke, so she gave them to me.

One of the things they did on the course was to have a sort of inspection parade, rather like they do in the army. They would check that your harness was in order, your grooming kit, lead and so on, all of which were kept in a box. I sneaked into Pete's room and put the knickers into his box.

The trainer went around and Pete had put his box up on the table with the others. The trainer told Pete to open his box.

'What the bloody hell's this?' he said, in front of everybody, holding up this pair of lady's knickers. Those of my friends who could see told me that Pete had a very red face.

'Get you for that one, Bollard,' he whispered as we were getting into the van

Pete and I kept in touch — I went over to visit him and he came to visit me. When I returned to Bray, and as I waited to start serious work with Ian, I often missed the crowd I'd got to know and like so much in Exeter — especially Pete. I still smile as I remember some of the tricks we played there.

* * *

I completed my training and it was a sad occasion, as well as a happy one. I had made such good friends. It was a chapter of my life that I'll always remember.

They couldn't fit five of us with five dogs on the plane, so I came home last. There was a tremendous thunderstorm all the way over during the flight — the plane did everything but fall apart. There were people screaming and people praying, but Ian was fast asleep under the seat.

Sarah's nephew met me with two of the boys who were thrilled to see the dog.

The trainer was to come and help me after I had had a few days to settle in. I let Ian explore the house and get to know it. We had been told to give the dogs twenty-four hours before putting them on the harness. I knew that my dog and I were going to be the centre of attention in Bray.

For quite a long time after I got home, I was followed everywhere by hordes of children. There would be perhaps one of my own sons and about twenty other children. They had never seen a guide dog before in Bray, and were agog at the sight of a man whom they'd always seen being led about by one of his boys going around on his own with a dog.

When I had been at home for a day, I decided I'd walk to the post office. I reached up for Ian's harness, and Sarah said that she would come with us.

'No, Sarah,' I said. 'I've just spent a hard month training — I've been through hell to get this dog and it's working. I haven't done all that so that you can take my arm and walk me round to the post office. I'll go on my own.'

I went out, told Ian what to do, and set off to go round the corner. I knew that Sarah was following me, because I could feel her eyes on my back, some way behind.

When I got to the post office, all the neighbours gathered round: 'Oh, Mr Bollard, on your own, with your dog. And here's Mrs Bollard coming behind you!'

* * *

After about a week, the trainer came over and we walked around the town. He asked me the places where I was likely to go, such as the bank, the church, the shops. He was happy with us and he went back, leaving me to fill out reports every week, telling him how my dog was behaving and mentioning any problems I might have. Then they would ring me and tell me how to deal with the difficulties. As it happened, I didn't have many problems with Ian — he was a very clever dog.

It was the greatest thrill, the greatest joy, to be able to say, 'I'm going for a walk on the sea front,' without having to ask if somebody would come with me. Just as Braille gave blind people literacy, so guide dogs gave us — certainly gave me — mobility and independence.

It's important to mention that guide dogs don't work for everybody. It takes a particular kind of person to work with a dog. You have to have a lot of trust and, in my early days, I didn't have that trust. To anyone who wonders whether a guide dog could be the answer for them, I would tell them to try it — better to try and fail than to go through life wondering if a guide dog would have been the answer for you.

Guide dogs aren't only for young people either — I know

an eighty-year-old who had a guide dog. So, if you are blind and reading this book, or having it read to you, and you think you'd like to give guide dogs a whirl, go for it. One of the best things that has ever happened to me is getting my guide dog, and I deeply, deeply regret that it didn't happen when I left the band and came to Bray. It would have saved me a lot of heart-ache and a lot of soul searching.

* * *

Ian and I went everywhere together. On one of our very first outings, I set out rather cautiously for the shops. It was a beautiful summer's day, and everything was going smoothly. I was so pleased with myself and Ian that I decided to take the long way home. Suddenly, the sun disappeared, and heavy clouds rolled up. Dressed as I was in light summer clothes, I urged Ian to go faster, and made for the nearest shelter which was our local church. As I rushed through the gate, heavy raindrops began to fall and there was a distant rumble of thunder.

I was inside the door and praising Ian when I heard a head-mistressy sort of voice: 'You can't bring that dog in here!'

'I didn't bring him in,' I replied. 'He brought me in.'

'This is a Catholic church.'

'That's okay, he's a Catholic dog.' I was beginning to see red — quite an achievement in my case.

'He's a guide dog,' I said. 'They're mentioned in the Bible — let me remind you. "He leadeth me along the right path, he is true to his name." In fact, if you spell "dog" backwards, he has more right to be here than either of us.'

She marched away, muttering something about blasphemy.

Ian didn't always behave so well though. I had a friend — a nun called Sister Mary Josephine whom I always called Rosaleen. She taught music at a large school for girls near Bray. I had composed a Mass for the girls' choir and they had performed it extremely well.

These girls were really excited about my guide dog — they had collected money and made a donation to the Guide Dogs for the Blind Association. I had promised that when I came home, I would bring Ian to the school to show him to them.

Rosaleen came with a car to collect me. The girls loved the dog and he was thrilled with being made a fuss of. I played the piano, we sang a few songs, and there was a great friendly atmosphere.

On the way home, Ian, getting over his excitement, decided to break wind. The smell in the car was unbelievable. I wound the window down. 'Oh, *Ian*,' I said.

'Thanks be to God, Joe,' said Sister Mary Josephine. 'I was afraid you might think it was me!' And she wound her window down too.

Ian never grew out of this habit, and he used to do it at the most awkward times — at choir practice, for instance. Another time, I was to be interviewed on radio by Jim Sherwin. Ian got under the table. All of a sudden, as we were talking about guide dogs and about my training, he produced one of his best.

'Phew. Stop the tape,' said Jim, and we started to laugh.

The producer came in from the control room, saying, 'What was all that about?' But as soon as he opened the door, he said, 'Oh, I know.'

* * *

When the time came for Ian to retire, I decided to keep him. I had the option of keeping him provided that I didn't allow him to work, and I hated the idea of parting with him. However, the effect on poor Ian was devastating. When I brought my new dog home and Ian was left behind while I took her with me, I think it broke his heart. He died quite soon afterwards.

The day that Ian retired, I felt bereft. I put my hand on his head and said to him, 'Thanks for everything old son, but all good things come to an end.' There were tears in my eyes, and I was sure I'd never get a dog like him again.

Finishing with your guide dog is a heartbreaking experience, but if you want to keep your independence and mobility, it has to happen. I would never keep a retired guide dog again. After years of faithful service, he has to watch while you put the harness on the new dog and bring it out each day. No wonder Ian moped and pined.

When Whiskey, my current dog, retires, she will go back to

the family who 'walked' her, and will have a wonderful home. Many guide dogs do this, and there is a list of suitable families waiting for retired dogs as family pets.

* * *

I've had two guide dogs since Ian — first Bridie then Whiskey — and that necessitated my going for training to Cork for a month each time. I went through the same things over again. Even though I knew the ropes, I was working with a new dog. I will have to do it again when Whiskey retires.

I thought Ian was good, but Whiskey is better. I think she was a human being in a previous incarnation. I'm going to be devastated when she retires. She works exceptionally well as a guide dog, she's a lovable pet, she loves life and loves people. I honestly don't think I'll ever get a dog as good as her.

In all the years that I've had a guide dog, I have only once been refused admission to a building. This was at the launch of a magazine about people with disabilities. The doorman refused me admission with my dog, but fortunately I knew a name to ask for and the matter was soon sorted out.

Taxis, however, are a different matter. I have often been refused by taxi drivers. I don't believe in making a fuss, feeling that if one driver won't take me, another will. The first time it happened, in central Dublin, I tried the first three drivers in a taxi rank, and all refused to take my guide dog. The fourth driver asked me what had happened and, when I told him, he got out of the cab and called the other three all the names he could think of. Then he said, 'Get into my cab.' I did and we drove away.

As we drove along, he gave me the number of the Taximens' Association to ring when I got home. I did this, explaining what had happened. I told them that the dog was a guide dog and would sit on the floor. The guy I was talking to said, 'Well, why didn't you take their numbers?'

'Now wait a minute,' I said. 'Whiskey is a very clever dog, but one thing she can't do is read.'

'... Oh. Yes. They do have the right to refuse you, you know.'

Not long afterwards, I was flying back from Birmingham. It was late, I was tired. I decided to take a cab from Dublin Airport to Bray — quite a lucrative run for a taximan. A friend took me out to the rank with my dog.

The first driver said, 'I don't take dogs.'

My friend protested on my behalf, but to no avail. A second driver also refused me. A third one came along — same story.

The fourth driver asked where I was going. I said Bray, and he agreed to take us.

'Why didn't the first three cabs take you?' asked the driver. 'Did they know where you were going?'

'No, they didn't give me the chance to tell them.'

'I'll tell you what,' said the taximan. 'If you'd said you were going to Bray from the airport, they'd have taken you if you'd had a hippopotamus with you.'

I have heard that some legislation is being introduced which will oblige taxi drivers to take guide dogs, but I have no details of this.

Perhaps the reason they refuse is that some blind people aren't as particular about their dogs as they might be. One driver said to me, 'If I carry somebody with a wet guide dog on a rainy day, and he lets it up on the seat, the next call I get may be to the Dáil to collect a TD's wife in a mink coat.'

Guide dogs are actually strictly trained not to get up on car seats, and no owner should allow their dog on the seats.

Now I forestall trouble by getting into the cab, beside the driver, pulling the dog in after me, and then telling him where I'm going. Once you're in, you're not getting out. This piece of advice was given to me by another taxi driver.

* * *

The Irish Guide Dogs' Association, now called Guide Dogs for the Blind, was formed in 1976. A meeting was called for all who were interested, and the association was formed by Mrs Mary Dunlop, who for years had worked as a fund-raiser for the British Guide Dogs for the Blind Association, along with a Mr Jim Dennehy, a blind person from Cork.

Although we had our first meeting in 1976, we didn't really

get off the ground until 1981 or 1982. Now, the association is doing well, and no longer does any blind person have any connection with the GDBA (the Guide Dogs for the Blind Association in England). The associations do exchange dogs and send bitches over to be mated with stud dogs, but no blind person goes to England for a dog now — we all go to Cork.

Nobody pays anything for a guide dog, either in Britain or at the Irish centre in Cork. This is so that nobody can say, 'I'd have a guide dog, but I can't afford one.' Guide Dogs for the Blind depends mainly on voluntary donations, although it does get some grant aid. Nowadays, when a blind person has completed his or her training and gets a guide dog, the dog is actually leased out at 5p a year. This gives the association the right to claim the dog back, should the blind person ill-treat it. This has never happened, as far as I am aware.

At the end of your course, you make a voluntary donation — it could be 50p, or it could be £50. The upkeep of your dog is subsidised by the association: its booster vaccinations are given free, and the vet who gives them is reimbursed by the various companies who produce animal medicines. Most vets are very good and if they charge anything at all for the dog's regular six-monthly visits, it's minimal.

Having a guide dog changed my life. I only wish I'd realised sooner what it would mean to me.

~ Twenty-One ~

When I brought Ian home from Exeter, Sarah, who had been so much against the idea of my having a guide dog, was completely won over by him. The snag was that she couldn't help feeding him titbits. When she was cooking, he would look up at her with his big, sad eyes, and lots of scraps would come his way. I would give out to her, but she'd say, 'I can't resist him.'

In the end, I wrote to the guide-dog people for advice, and they suggested that I should give Sarah a dog of her own. I asked around, and found that a lady who bred pedigree chihuahuas had a show animal, which she was prepared to give away, provided that it wasn't used for breeding purposes.

The little dog arrived, and Ian had no time at all for him. I think he thought he was a cat. Very soon, Sarah had acquired not one, but three, chihuahuas. She loved these little dogs which were her pets, and they were very little trouble, as running upstairs and downstairs seemed to give them as much exercise as they needed. So from having no dogs, we finished up having four.

That's how it happened that Sarah and I, the three boys, Ian and three chihuahuas set off for England on a holiday. It took a great deal of persuasion before Sarah would agree to go. She is a bad traveller and she won't fly, but I had told the boys so much about England, especially Liverpool, that I was really anxious to bring them there. So we went to stay with my sister Sue for a week.

My mother had visited us several times, so the boys knew their granny. One of my brothers had also been to see us with his wife, but they didn't know their other uncles, aunts and cousins, and were looking forward to meeting them.

We went by bus and boat and train, and I remember the lads' excitement as we travelled along the north coast of Wales to Chester. There, Sue met us by car, and there was another thrill — going under the Mersey tunnel into Liverpool. It was the first time we had been away as a family, and I intended to make the most of it. I wanted them to have boyhood memories of this family holiday. In Liverpool, I brought them to a soccer match to see Everton play, and to many of my old haunts.

One of Sarah's reasons for not wanting to go away was that she was afraid that the house would be burgled. We asked a neighbour to keep an eye on it for us, but when we arrived home at about eight in the morning the house had been burgled. Our neighbour had disturbed the burglar and he had run away. My radio was missing, but nothing else of value.

* * *

When I left the Ernie Pigott Group, I worked for a while as a freelance musician, getting gigs here and there.

One night, I got a call from a singer/MC to do a gig at the Dalkey Island Hotel. I duly went over and we had a reasonably good night — it was August with plenty of tourists. Jim Delaney, the owner of the hotel, was impressed. After the gig, he asked me to take on the job one night a week.

I agreed. One night a week became two nights, and about a month later, Jim offered me a permanent job. I worked at the Dalkey Island Hotel from Wednesday to Sunday night every week for thirteen years, and people still remind me of the 'good old days' there.

Dalkey was a bit of a nuisance to get to, but Ian was giving me more confidence all the time, as well as more independence.

The Dalkey Island lounge was much bigger than the one at The Silver Tassie. It could hold up to 450 people. At first, I just sang and played in this lounge, but after a few years, they were doing some renovations and they built a little stage for me in the corner by the bar.

What I was playing wasn't anything extraordinary, but it was what people seemed to want. It was a throw-back to my showband days, when we impersonated the singers of the time, and the band did 'cover versions' of the hit records of the day. Now at the Dalkey Island, the patrons wanted to hear Nat King Cole songs sung like Nat King Cole, Roy Orbison songs sung like Roy Orbison. They didn't want to hear Joe Bollard at all. Occasionally I got to sing in my own voice but it was rare.

The Dalkey Island was rapidly becoming the place to be, especially on Sunday nights when we had our sing-along for an hour or an hour and a half. Saturdays weren't quite as good, but the hotel was well-known for its weddings, and many guests who didn't want to go to the disco, came up to the lounge instead.

When I started there, the organ wasn't great, but Jim Delaney surprised me one day by sending me out to buy a new one. I went out and fell in love with a fantastic keyboard. However, I nearly died when I heard that it cost £4,000 — a huge sum in the 1970s. However, when I told Jim Delaney about this, he just said, 'Get it.' So I did.

It was a tremendous instrument, I could get all sorts of sounds on it and it was marvellous for doing impressions — now I could imitate the voices of the hit singers and also the backings on their records.

I had become an institution, and the Dalkey Island was packing them in. Everything was going my way, but a couple of years after I started, I was to have a bitter disappointment, and two more were to follow.

* * *

In 1977, I heard, through the grapevine, that RTÉ was going to run a training course for blind people, with the possibility that they might take part in radio. There was a radio programme called *Listen and See*, for and about blind and visually impaired people, which went out on a Sunday. For many years, blind people had been asking that the programme be presented by a blind or visually impaired person. RTÉ, on the other hand, wanted the programme to be presented by a professional journalist, but with some input by blind people.

When I heard about the course, I immediately rang up and enquired about it. It would run for ten mornings, and was to begin the following Monday morning at nine o'clock.

There were three of us on the course. One of the others was the present Chief Executive Officer of the National Council for the Blind, Des Kenny. The other was a guy called Glen Langston, who is now working in America. All three of us were totally blind.

We found the first day very basic. The first thing they showed us was a cassette recorder, one of which I'd had for the previous fifteen or sixteen years. We spent an hour learning how to fast forward and rewind, and how to insert a microphone. We were sent home that afternoon with instructions to write a five-minute script on a subject of our choice. The following day we were going to do voice tests.

I wrote my script, on 'Getting Your Song Published', as I was doing a lot of songwriting at the time. We were called in alphabetical order, so I went into the studio first.

I sat down, put the cans (earphones) on and they said to me, 'Joe, you can start when the red light comes on.'

A lady's voice said, 'Oh. Sure he won't be able to see the red light.' Then she said to me, 'You can start when I wave to you through the window.'

'Unless you have a bell in your hand,' I said, 'I won't know when you wave. Surely to goodness — I can't do an awful lot, but I can count three to go.'

At the end of the course, we had to make up a twenty-minute magazine. Mine was about work done by blind people. We finished, and they said, 'We'll let you know.'

It was three or four months before I heard any more. I received a letter telling me that my voice was totally unsuitable for radio. I was shattered. It was one of the biggest disappointments of my life. It took me right back to the time when I didn't get to Worcester College on my scholarship. I sat there, dumbfounded, and moped for three days. I *knew* that I was good enough. I couldn't believe it.

Then it suddenly occurred to me to try to prove them wrong. I began to recover my self-esteem, and to look out for some kind of work in radio.

* * *

I got my chance to prove myself when there was a public meeting in the Royal Hotel in Bray. Pirate radio stations were springing up all over the country, and Bray wanted its own station.

I went to this meeting, having made up my mind that I wasn't going to be put down because of my blindness or for any other reason. I marched in, told the man in the chair I'd had training with RTÉ, and went on to give him all sorts of details of experience with the BBC and other work I'd done here and there.

'I'll do the very first programme,' I told him. 'And I'll do a programme every day from eleven to one, which will be called *Morning Mixture*. It will be lots of easy listening, relaxing music, with plenty of local notices thrown in.'

I must have spoken very persuasively. Nobody asked how I was going to read the notices or how I was going to manage. Instead, when I had finished, they just said, 'Right Joe — you go ahead and do it.'

On 22 August 1979, together with my good friend Mark Quinn, one of the instigators of the radio station, I walked down from my house with a bag of records. I had all sorts of notices written out, stolen from the local newspaper. I sat down at the desk, and Mark did the mixing — playing the records while I did the spiel in between.

Our station was called BLB, Bray Local Broadcasting, and I think we had a range of about three miles. We were on the medium wave, and we were lucky to get as far as Shankill.

Those first pirate days were really horrendous. We would put records on at the wrong speed and we would forget to close the microphone. People wanted to get in on the act who had had no training of any sort. Many seemed to think they were broadcasting to the world, rather than a three-mile radius. Most of us were on ego trips.

One woman came down to do her very first radio programme dressed in her fur coat and all her jewellery. Her programme followed mine. She was shaking like a leaf when she came on in all her finery. She was so nervous that it sounded really bad. In fact, she was so nervous that she wet her knickers and there was a big puddle under the chair!

Eventually, we learned to 'mix' for ourselves — that is, to play the records as well as do the chat. While one record is playing, you cue the next one up. Then you talk, and then you switch the record on. The prime fault that everyone was guilty of was forgetting to switch the microphone off. We mostly brought our own records in with us, though we did have a small library of discs we'd bought for the station. We ran little functions to raise money to buy a new transmitter, and to increase our record library.

On one occasion a DJ played a few records. Then she needed to go to the library to get The Carpenters, which was her next record. She said to somebody, 'Would you go out and get me The Carpenters while the Roger Whittaker record is playing?'

But whoever it was forgot. The DJ switched on her microphone and said, 'That was Roger Whittaker. The time on Bray Local Broadcasting is four minutes past two, and now we have for you The Carpenters.'

She reached over and there was no Carpenters on the other turntable. Forgetting to bring down her microphone, she shouted, 'JESUS! Where's The Carpenters? *JESUS*!! I told you to get the bloody Carpenters.'

Of course, everybody was listening to this over the air, and someone outside realised and dashed into the studio, and as he did, she turned around and said, 'I told her to bring me in The Carpenters.'

He brought down her microphone and, realising what had happened, she cried bitter tears and got up off the chair and went home. Someone else had to finish up the programme.

However, in spite of everything, the station just took off. Those were the days of learning radio. We weren't being paid, but we all got on together: it was community radio at its best. I didn't mind not being paid. It was a tremendous time in my life. In addition to my work at the Dalkey Island, I was getting a thrill from presenting my programme, from preparing it beforehand and from doing something for the community.

Local people thought I was good — the researchers had worked out that my programme had a listening audience of 75,000 — and I had the joy of playing the records that I loved, and talking to the people that I loved. Lots of top stars from the cabaret scene came out to be interviewed. If they didn't come to the studio, I'd take off in the afternoon with my tape recorder and go and interview them. Only my friends knew that I was blind — I never mentioned it on the air.

Once I was advertising a church-gate collection for Guide Dogs for the Blind, and I happened to use the words, 'We guide-dog owners....'

After the programme I was called to the phone. A lady's voice said, 'Are you the Joe Bollard who's just been on air?'

I said that I was.

'You were talking about guide dogs.'

'Yes, there's a collection on Sunday.'

'But you said you were a guide-dog owner.'

'I am a guide-dog owner.'

'But they're only for blind people,' she said. 'Are you blind?'

'Yes, of course, love,' I said. 'Are you surprised?'

'Yes,' she replied. 'You don't talk blind.'

~ Twenty-Two ~

Like all good things, it had to come to an end. The government decided to put all pirate radio stations off the air, including ours. We came back on again as Horizon Radio, which was professional, so we expected to be paid. It was agreed that if we worked the first six months for nothing, the daytime presenters would be paid. However, the station soon found itself in dire straits and couldn't pay us.

A new (paid) controller was brought in, and he decided that certain changes had to be made. He asked me to change my time of eleven–one o'clock to two hours earlier. By that time, I had started to play and sing at funerals, which was a way of earning my living, and I didn't want to give it up for unpaid work. Finally, however, I agreed, on the understanding that, after three months, I would be put on a salary. However, at the end of three months the funds still weren't there. I asked for my old slot back, but was refused.

I knew there had to be some reason for this. Then, one day, I happened to be in a room at the radio station, and I heard someone in the next room say, 'If you want this radio station to be more popular, you'll have to get rid of Joe Bollard. It gives the station a bad image, using an old, blind man.'

I went back to Mr Heffernan, the controller, and asked him once again about the situation. He repeated that I couldn't be paid and that I couldn't have my old slot back.

The following day, I went on air and told my listeners that this would be my last week with Horizon Radio — that I no longer wished to work with the station. The switchboard lit up with phone calls, but I had decided to give no reasons. That afternoon, my own phone never stopped ringing as listeners wanted to know why I was finishing. I replied that it was a personal matter. Then the newspapers rang me and a reporter said that I owed it to my listeners to tell them why.

I slept on it, and the following morning I made an announcement on my programme: 'The reason I'm finishing on Friday is that the management of this radio station reneged on a promise that they made and I can no longer work under the present conditions.'

Dave Heffernan rang me up that evening. He said that I had broken some Wireless Telegraphy Act. 'You leave me with no option but to tell you not to bother coming into the radio station again,' he finished up.

So I had done my last programme. People wanted to demonstrate but I wouldn't hear of it.

It was the end of another era.

Two weeks later, the producer of the radio programme *Listen and See* asked me if I'd be interested in joining RTÉ as a reporter for the programme. I gratefully accepted, and have also since presented five radio documentaries.

* * *

All this time, I was playing and singing at the Dalkey Island Hotel. If anything, the crowds were bigger than ever. It was a time I'll never forget.

Over the years, the patrons had become friends. I knew most of the regulars. On Sunday nights, during the last hour, some of them would get up and actually dance in the middle of the floor, or in the lounge, or just around the stage. There was a Joe Bollard Fan Club, and at Christmas and my birthday, they would load me with presents. A couple of times, we tried cabaret, bringing in some well-known people, particularly during the Dalkey Festival, which was in July.

One Sunday night, when the place was thronged, someone told me that there was a group of fifty Liverpool policemen there — guests of the local gardaí. Having spent most of my childhood in Liverpool, I began to sing a few Liverpool songs. The place went into uproar. At the end of the night, although I'm an Everton supporter, I sang the Liverpool football anthem, 'You'll Never Walk Alone'. Nearly 500 people, crammed into the lounge, stood up, with their hands above their heads, singing. It was tremendous.

Afterwards, I had a long chat with the policemen and I told them where my mother lived in Liverpool. Shortly after they returned, they visited her and presented her with flowers and chocolates, saying that her son had really made their weekend.

* * *

The end was sudden and sad.

On a Sunday night in 1988, when I was preparing to go to the Dalkey Island, I was in the shower when the phone rang and I was told that Jim Delaney wanted me quickly. So I jumped out, wrapped the towel around me and, still dripping water, I took the call. I thought he wanted me to make some announcement during the course of the night.

'What is it you want?' I asked.

'Joe, I'm just ringing you to ask you to inform the patrons that tonight will be our last night for music. We're no longer having music in the hotel.'

I thought he was pulling my leg at first. I said, 'And where does that leave me?'

'You're good enough — you'll find work.' I knew that there were going to be renovations in the hotel, but didn't know any details. His words came as a total shock.

At nine o'clock, when the place was full, I made the announcement. There was a sort of disbelieving pause for about ten seconds and then all hell broke loose. There were only two junior barmen on that night, and everyone rushed over to the bar, wanting to know why. The barmen couldn't give them any answer and neither could I.

As when I lost my job with Horizon Radio, my fans planned a demonstration outside the hotel for the following weekend, but I said I would prefer if they didn't. I was angry and hurt, but I prefer to keep my feelings to myself.

Now there are plans to demolish the hotel and build a huge apartment block. There are objections to this plan, so it may never happen.

After I left, there were several years of marking time. Playing at the Dalkey Island for thirteen years was in many ways a good thing, but it was bad in that it had taken me off the cabaret scene. People in my area knew where I was working and that there was a Joe Bollard Fan Club, but my work was local. Elsewhere I wasn't well-known, and, as I'd been away from cabaret for thirteen years, it was assumed that either I was dead or that I wasn't working any more.

When I left, I naturally went around Bray and made it known that I was looking for work — cabaret, nightclubs and gigs. I suddenly and desperately needed the work, but there was none forthcoming. It hurt because I had lived in Bray for years and was well-known there.

Funeral work was another story. Not long after I left the Dalkey Island, somebody asked me to sing at his grandmother's funeral, because she loved my singing. After the Mass, the funeral directors approached me to ask whether I would be interested in singing at more funerals. We agreed terms and procedure. At first it crept, but now it has snowballed and I sing and play at a great many funerals in Wicklow and south Co. Dublin. Funeral work has its advantages. It takes only about an hour, so you don't have to sit for ages in a smoky atmosphere. Also, you get the chance to sing some great music, and you get paid well. In fact, it may sound strange, but if I had the chance, I would do nothing else.

* * *

During the 1980s, my great interest in soccer was reviving. Our local team, Bray Wanderers, joined the League of Ireland in 1985, and most Sundays, Noel, Declan and I would take off down to the Carlisle grounds to support our team. People soon got used to the blind man at the matches, and I joined the Supporters Club and got to know the lads on the team, especially goalkeeper Josh Moran. I also got to know the manager, Pat Devlin, who has been a good friend of mine ever since.

In 1990, Bray Wanderers reached the FAI Cup Final where they played St Francis. The whole of Wicklow must have been at Landsdowne Road for the match. With two minutes to go, Wanderers were winning three–nil. Noel and I went down to the fence at the side of the field and I said, 'When the final whistle blows, I want to get over onto the pitch and go and find Josh Moran — I want to be first on the pitch.'

'Dad, when you go over the fence, the goal's on your left, Josh is on your left,' Noel told me. 'There's nothing you can run into.'

As soon as the referee blew the whistle, I jumped over the fence and ran the whole length of the pitch. Josh saw me coming and ran towards me and we hugged and jumped up and down. There were pictures in the papers the next day of this blind man flying down the pitch. For me though, being blind didn't come into it. Our local team, of which I was so proud, had won the FAI Cup, and I still get butterflies in my tummy when I think of it.

* * *

By the time I found myself unemployed, the two older boys had grown up and left home, and Declan was shortly to go too. I was very lucky with the boys — they got work and weren't unemployed for any length of time. If they were out of work, they didn't sit back and let it happen but went out looking for jobs. Now all three are married. Joseph and his wife and children live just three doors away from us, while Noel and his family, and Declan and his wife are living in Greystones, a few miles down the coast.

They were never musical to the extent that I am, although all three enjoy listening to music. They love sports though, and that is perhaps the chief way in which they are like me. It was a great joy to sing and play at all of their weddings. I have six grandchildren — perhaps one of them will follow in their grandfather's footsteps.

Joseph is still a bus-driver, Noel works in the head office of ESB, and Declan works in a dry-cleaning establishment in Greystones.

I'm grateful for my three boys. They are very good to us, supporting and helping us in every way they can.

* * *

Although I no longer had children and school fees to worry about, money was scarce. I was getting little bits of work here and there — some funerals and private functions — but things were tough. In 1988, Des Kenny, the Chief Executive Officer of the National Council for the Blind, asked me to become editor of a magazine called *Scéal Beo*, which means the living word, or story. It was a free magazine, sent out monthly on cassette to blind people throughout Ireland.

When I took over, very few people were receiving it. I asked permission to do things my way, and was told, 'Fair enough, within reason.'

My aims were to get the magazine out fortnightly, and to keep to the subjects of blindness, visual impairment and disabilities generally, but to make it livelier. I got permission to do that, and the magazine took off immediately. The mailing list went up from about ninety-six to nearly a thousand.

It requires a lot of work. I have total control over input into the magazine, but must always remember that it is the official organ of the NCBI and my personal views must not take precedence over those of the NCBI.

I have been editing the magazine for nearly ten years now, and it is a job I really enjoy.

~ Twenty-Three ~

In 1991, I was in P.V. Doyle House, the headquarters of the National Council for the Blind, standing at the reception desk, when I felt this big hand on my shoulder, and a booming voice said, 'I presume you're Joe Bollard.'

I said that I was, and he introduced himself as Eamon Duffy. He had been appointed official fund-raising co-ordinator for the NCBI.

'I have some very innovative ideas for fund-raising,' he told me. 'How would you like to come to America with me?'

I didn't really take him very seriously. But he brought me into the office to talk and asked, 'How are you on tandems?'

He explained that he had this idea for a fund-raising cycle from San Francisco to Los Angeles — 500 miles — if I could just find someone to ride on the front of my tandem.

'Wait a minute,' I said. 'I've got to find the tandem first.'

He brushed this aside. 'Find yourself a tandem, then. And if you can come up with £3,000, you can be on this cycle.'

Going home on the DART, my initial thought was that the man was crazy. But the more I thought about the idea, the more I liked it. I wondered who to ask to go on the front of the bike (which I didn't have), and eventually I approached a friend from my pirate-radio days, Nick Eoghan.

'Great idea,' he said. 'Let's give it a go.'

We found a tandem after some time, and I went back to Eamon Duffy.

'Right, Eamon, you're on,' I said. 'Tell us what we have to do now.'

'You have to go out and raise £3,000 each.'

'Good God. I thought it was £3,000 between us.'

I got back to Nick, and we decided to raise the money. Fergus O'Hagan gave our cycling club its name, the 'Blazing Saddles'. We raised money with cabarets, bingo and coffee mornings. It was difficult, but local people in Bray were very helpful in supporting whatever fund-raising ventures we got up to.

Meanwhile we had begun training — it was good fun, but the tandem was a wreck. How we were to get from San Francisco to Los Angeles on it, I had no idea. I had also got an exercise bike and put in hours on that. My first problem was my bum. It objected strongly to the pressure and certainly wouldn't have agreed with Jack Charlton's policy, 'Keep them under pressure'! I spent a small fortune on Vaseline and didn't appreciate the comment of a friend who, when I asked him for advice, suggested that I 'start from the bottom'.

At last, our training was complete, the money was raised, and we were ready to set off for San Francisco.

* * *

On Friday, 15 March 1992, we set off — a hundred cyclists, their back-up team and supporters. I had one thing in common with Columbus, five centuries before: neither of us knew what was in store.

We alighted in San Francisco to the sound of bagpipes. There was a reception committee to meet us. We were tired but excited, and when we had checked in at our hotel, we were given our itinerary for the following day.

At that point, we met Larry Shapiro, our cycling co-ordinator for the trip. I found him an enigma: he seemed to combine the dictatorship of President Gadaffi, the off-beat humour of Woody Allen, the stubbornness of Margaret Thatcher and the imagination of Walter Mitty. Add to that his ability to keep up a non-stop patter, his inability to calculate mileage, his concern for the riders, his admiration for the blind cyclists and his total disbelief that any of us would finish the trip — and you have Larry Shapiro. I took an instant dislike to him, but as the trip progressed, I did mellow towards him somewhat.

We hadn't come equipped for rain, but it poured while we were in San Francisco. On St Patrick's Day, we attended the parade, which was enormous, colourful and noisy. The elements disregarded Barbra Streisand's plea, 'Don't rain on my parade', and we were soaked, but we didn't care. One man grabbed me in a bear hug and asked whether I knew Seán Doran in Newcastle West, and to be sure and tell him Pat was asking after him!

The following day, we took to the road in the rain. It wasn't too heavy when we set off, but a few miles into our 70-mile journey, the skies opened and it bucketed down. We had also had a problem with a valve. It didn't delay us long, but we were left behind, and we got lost. We had gone three miles out of our way before one of the party came to rescue us.

Later on, the sun appeared for a while and we could hear the sound of the Pacific Ocean washing on the beach on our right. The air was fresh and sweet, and I got a great feeling of exhilaration. Tired but happy on our arrival at the Seacliff Hotel, I had a swim in the pool, a good meal, and fell asleep in a lovely soft bed.

For the next couple of days we cycled close to the coast and I recall the strong fish smell from the sea. The breeze carried the aroma of trees, and the earth smelt damp after the heavy rain. I was enjoying myself, but we were having trouble with the gears on the tandem. We arrived at Carmel, where Larry Shapiro told us that the following day would be the toughest of the trip. It would be 90 miles, climbing all the time, to a height of 5,000 feet.

The road is called the Big Sur and leads up to Hearst Castle. Mountains rose straight up from the road on our left; on the right was the Pacific, a sheer thousand feet below. Nick couldn't look down. At one point, I stopped the bike and sat on the low wall which kept us from hurtling down to the rocks below. I just sat there with my legs hanging over the edge while Nick hung onto my tee shirt.

'Stop messing about, Joe,' he said. 'On your bike again.'

We reached our destination, San Simone, exhausted, but feeling that, after Big Sur, the rest of the trip would be a doddle.

The following day, we heard with horror that our tandem was no longer roadworthy. This was Larry Shapiro's decision and we had to abide by it. At San Louis Obispo we found a bicycle shop and explained our dilemma. The owner lent us a tandem for the rest of our journey to Los Angeles. We were flabbergasted. He told us that his father was blind and that he was delighted to be of service to any organisation for the blind. And anyway, he said, he loved the Irish.

On Friday, we reached Solvang, a lovely little town which was settled by the Danes. There are little Scandinavian houses, and lots of curiosity shops selling clocks, musical boxes and trinkets, while the food is mainly Danish, with good cheese and bacon. The main shopping centre is called Copenhagen, and it's straight out of Hans Christian Andersen.

It was an unpleasant contrast moving onto Highway 101 on our way to Santa Barbara. The traffic was very frightening and the truck drivers had little regard for cyclists. Some of those Juggernauts came so close, they almost took the suntan lotion off my leg.

The next morning, Sunday, I had one of the most memorable experiences of the trip, as one hundred cyclists paraded on their bikes to the old Mission at Santa Barbara. We attended Mass at this lovely old building which has unusually high windows. The priest told us that the windows were high to prevent the Indians from shooting their arrows through at the worshippers in the early days of the Mission. It was a plain wooden rectangular church with an atmosphere all its own. I played the organ, while another blind cyclist sang a hymn he had written especially for the occasion. I shall never forget how beautiful the choir was, and how moving the Mass. I felt honoured to be part of it.

Before the last stage of our journey, we stayed at Ventura, where we took part in a fancy-dress competition. We had to improvise, and I decided that Nick and I would dress as Arabs. With the help of sheets and pillowcases from our hotel bedroom, Nick dressed as Sheikh Rattle and Roll while I was Blind Ali. We paraded with an assortment of nuns, pirates, priests, tarts and pop stars. It was great fun.

Then came the last leg of our tour. We kept together in one

group as we headed towards the finish with a police escort. The freeway had been closed off for only the third time in American history. The other occasions were the Grand Prix and the Americas Cup. With the tandems leading the cyclists, we broke the finishing tape at Long Beach, while the sun shone, the band played, and the *Queen Mary* sounded her siren in our honour.

I jumped off the bike and hugged my pilot and good friend Nick, or Pontius the pilot, as I called him. We had been through some tough times but he had been both an inspiration to me, and a fun person to be with. He was one of the best pilots I have had.

* * *

The following year, the Blazing Saddles went to Florida. Our cycle was from Miami to Fort Lauderdale. It wasn't as tough as our Californian trip as regards the terrain, but it was desperately hot, which made it most exhausting. Unfortunately, Nick couldn't accompany me on this cycle, so my pilot was a young man called Barry Gallagher.

While in Florida, I managed to do quite a lot of work for the magazine, *Scéal Beo*, and for the programme *Listen and See*, because I met and interviewed many people connected with the world of the blind. It was very interesting to learn about blind people in another continent — how they coped, how they lived, what was available for them. It was a good trip, and a strenuous one.

In 1994, we had our biggest expedition to date. It took place in Australia, and we cycled north from Sydney to Brisbane — a journey of 900 miles. I realised that I was going to need a good bike and a good pilot, and I was going to have to put in a lot of training.

As there was no question of getting a new bike, I had my old one overhauled and reconditioned from top to bottom. When it had been serviced, I found a good pilot called Jack Mackin. I really enjoyed our training programme tough though it was.

My joy was to go up to Roundwood on a summer's morning. I'd like to live there if ever I retire. Jack would come to my house, we'd check our gear and away we'd go up the long hill. We took the back road into Greystones, through Kilcoole, on to Ashford, backroads all the way, then turn right and up the Devil's Glen. Having left the traffic behind us, we could feel the peace, and hear the larks singing. I could hear the little streams flowing as we rode across them. Then there were the country smells — even slurry is a healthy smell. At the top of the five-mile drag, Jack would say that he could see the reservoir. Then we'd go down through the forest, sensing all the different smells — things you'd never notice in a car.

I have often been asked what I would choose to see if I had my sight, and I'd have to say, the beauty of the Wicklow Mountains. It might seem strange that I don't say, 'My wife and family,' but I know them — I know them so well that it doesn't matter to me what they look like. No, it would be the Wicklow Mountains or the Great Wall of China or the Everton team coming out onto the pitch at Goodison Park.

* * *

Our training stood to us in Australia, and we survived. Coordination is vital on a tandem, and when you get on or off, you have to get it right — otherwise you fall. Jack and I had developed a certain rapport, which was most important on hills. Jack would grade the hills, and when we were coming to one, he would say, 'This is a one, going into a two', or 'This one's a three going into a four.' He would let me know whether it was a long drag or a 50-yards dash.

There were some very long drags in Australia — long, long drags in undulating country. Then, in the mountains, it could be a six or a seven — even an eight, which is like going up a wall. When we started pedalling, Jack would tell me when he was changing gear, and when we got to the top, he had a word which meant 'stop pedalling and shut up' — 'FREE!' he would say, and I'd put my head on his bum, bring my elbows and knees in, and away we'd go.

For a blind person to get the feeling of movement, the wind against him, and of course the speed, is a real thrill. You have to have confidence, but I knew that Jack was in full control.

There were real hills in Australia, and we got 51 m.p.h. coming down one of them. Then we'd be on the level again, recovering and listening to the songs of the birds.

Australia was a great experience, and I was sad at having to part with Jack on our next trip, which took us half way around Europe in 1995.

~ Twenty-Four ~

Our European trip was very different from those that had gone before. We left Dublin on Saturday, 2 September 1995. We travelled to Budapest via London, and arrived in mid-afternoon only to find that most of our luggage was still in London.

Our spirits were not dampened though. Our luggage arrived on the next flight, and early on Sunday morning, we were taken on a tour of the city. My notion of Budapest had been of a drab, secretive town, but I was wrong. It is a spacious city, with large Baroque-style buildings, similar to those in Vienna.

We began our cycle the following day, leaving our hotel with a police escort, in heavy rain. The tandems had to stay in the rear for security reasons — perhaps they thought we were gangsters. My pilot was Kevin Boylan, and we got on really well. He was a quiet man, as unlike me as possible, and I had total confidence in him.

We cycled 80 miles that day, stopping for food at 42 miles. We were cold, wet through and miserable. When we'd eaten and set off again, the wind increased to gale force.

We arrived in Gyor at about three o'clock in the afternoon, soaked through. There is a lot of mining in this part of Hungary, and the dust is thrown into the air by the blasting, so when it rains, it rains black drops. When we reached our hotel, we immediately had to clean all our cycling gear.

The morning was dry, and we set off for Bratislava in bright sunshine. In Hungary, you feel that the country is just getting over the Communist régime. The farms are small, with lots of Russian cars and tractors. Maize and sunflowers grow in the fields by the road.

Having crossed the border into Slovakia, the terrain was flat, and there was a great atmosphere among us. We arrived in Bratislava to the sound of trams clanging through busy streets. One cyclist caught the wheel of her bike in the tramlines and came down heavily. Luckily her helmet took most of the force, as her head hit the ground, but she was badly shaken and was taken to hospital. She was released later in the afternoon. Another cyclist sprained his arm when he came down in the tramlines.

The Danube at Bratislava is far from blue — they tell me it's rather a dirty brown. Probably it was blue in Johann Strauss's day — 'The Brown Danube Waltz' doesn't have quite the same ring, somehow.

The Slovakian unit of currency is the Crona, but most of us had Deutschmarks which are also acceptable there. A beer cost only the equivalent of about 30p, but going to the loo cost 10p. Our group joked about having one beer or going to the loo three times in an evening. As I speak German, the second language in Slovakia, I was engaged as interpreter for the evening. I have never ordered so many drinks in my life.

On Wednesday, we left early, heading for Vienna. We crossed the Austrian border just three miles from Bratislava, and cycled through lovely Austrian villages with the sun shining and the birds singing. I was really elated, looking forward to getting to Vienna where we were to watch the soccer match between Ireland and Austria.

Suddenly, there was a grinding sound, and Kevin brought the bike to a halt. We pulled over to the side of the road and waited for our maintenance crew. When they examined the bike, we heard the worst — we had broken the back axle, so we had to travel to Vienna in the support vehicle. I was shattered.

The cyclists were accompanied into Vienna by a huge police escort, with horns blaring and flags waving. They were cheered on by Irish soccer supporters over for the match — which Ireland lost by three goals to one.

The following day, we were on the bike again. The maintenance crew had done a quick repair job, but our maintenance manager, Fintan McGill, told us to take it easy as the bike was just holding together, though quite safe. We set out for Maria

Taferl, about 64 miles, travelling rather gingerly and staying at the back of the group in case anything went wrong.

After a while, we heard a rattle and got off the bike. When Fintan arrived, he said that it needed open-heart surgery on the spot. He got us going, but we were far behind the others, and soon got lost, having missed a road sign. We were down an Austrian boreen, so we cycled through a courtyard, along the side of a house and out through the front gate, along another boreen and into a little village. We were in Moulln.

'This is where I think we should be,' I told Kevin. 'We must go to Krems.' I asked some children the way and they told us to turn left over the bridge and carry on for 30 kilometres.

We crossed the Danube and headed along a major road. Cars hooted at us and, thinking that they recognised us from the media coverage, I waved to them with a smile. After ten miles of this, Kevin said, in his quiet way, 'I don't think we should be here, Joe. A motorist has just shaken his fist at us.'

We carried on until we reached an emergency phone box. I lifted the shutter on the front and a stern voice shouted, 'Hallo!'

I tried to explain our position, and asked that the hotel where we were to stay should be told that Kevin and Joe were lost but safe. The voice told us to stay where we were.

After twenty minutes spent sitting on the side of the road, with the bike leaning against the fence, I tried the phone again, and the voice shouted, 'Didn't I tell you to stay there?' So I sat down again.

The police arrived ten minutes later. 'I am going to fine you 500 Austrian schillings (about £30) each, for riding on the Bundesstraße,' said the officer.

'We weren't cycling,' I lied.

'What's that?' He pointed to the tandem.

'It's broken. We've come from Moulln.'

'If you didn't cycle, how did you get here?'

Again I lied: 'We walked.'

'There's a fine of 500 schillings for walking on the Bundesstraße.'

'We didn't walk on the road.'

'Moulln is 20 kilometres from here,' said the policeman. 'If you didn't walk and you didn't cycle, how did you get here?'

'We walked on the grass verge.' (Another lie.)

'Where are you from?'

'Ireland,' I said.

'Ah,' said the policeman. 'Austria 3, Ireland 1.'

Great, I thought, he likes football. I began to talk about the match, and soon we were discussing the techniques and merits of the teams. We chatted for ten minutes and he said, 'Forget about the fines — you suffered enough at the hands of our international team last night. Where are you going?'

'Krems,' I said.

With that, he stepped onto the road, flagged down a passing truck, and yelled at the driver, 'Where are you going?'

'Krems,' was the frightened reply.

'Well, take these men and their bike with you.'

He helped to load the tandem and he whispered to me that I should give the driver a tip. As we drove away, he shouted after us, 'Next time it will be Austria 5, Ireland nil.' I waved and shook my head.

'Jesus,' said the driver as he drove away. 'I'm supposed to drive at 70 kilometres on this road, and when I was stopped I was doing 90. I thought he'd have me for speeding.'

'The Irish have brought you luck,' I said.

* * *

Maria Taferl, when at last we got there, turned out to be the most picturesque village you could imagine. Our hotel was at the top of a steep hill, and we cyclists sat out of doors in the warm evening sunshine, exchanging accounts of the day's events.

It was drizzling next morning as we set off for Linz, and we had to be careful coming down the steep hill, which had lots of hairpin bends and was very slippery. But the sun came out as we rode through the village, the church bells rang, and I was reminded of the opening moments of *The Sound of Music*.

Linz was the halfway point of the tour, and we were greeted with great media coverage. It had grown extremely hot and we were tired, but there was a lot of standing around for photo sessions. Later there were celebrations — it was a long day.

On Saturday, we reached Munich. This was a rest day, and in the evening we were entertained by the staff at Fiddler's Green, the biggest Irish pub in Munich. We headed for bed in the small hours, having enjoyed a great evening.

We cycled all day on Sunday, reaching Innsbruck around five o'clock in the afternoon. Outside our hotel, the local band, dressed in their colourful national costume, entertained us with cheerful Tyrolean 'oompah-oompah' music. Some of us had picked up a tummy bug, others were feeling the strain, but our spirits were still high. The ride through the Brenner Pass was planned for the following day, taking us over the Alps into Italy.

We left Innsbruck early, with our usual police escort. It was a real struggle pedalling over those tough hills. On our right was a solid wall of rock reaching up into the mountains. On our left, a motorway was built on huge pillars — an amazing construction. Having climbed for some time, the terrain levelled out for a while, then became steep again. We arrived at the top of the Brenner Pass shortly before noon. As we sat down at the food stop, the church bells rang out, as if to celebrate that we had conquered the pass.

It was considered too dangerous for the tandems to attempt the very steep descent to Bolzano, but we were adamant that we should be allowed to complete the trip, and objected in the strongest of terms to the management, who finally relented and allowed us to join the rest of the group. The descent was, however, hair-raising. Tremendous skill and strength were required to prevent our bikes from running away. As we passed through long tunnels under the mountains, the air became warmer and the wind less strong. We didn't see much of Bolzano, arriving late in the evening and, after a celebration dinner, going exhausted to bed.

Leaving Bolzano the following morning, with our police escort piloting us through the city traffic, we started the 100-mile ride to Verona. There were some nasty hills on this run, and it was hot, but the bike was going well and it was a good day to be on one. As we travelled through vineyards, Kevin and I could smell the grapes, then we went on through apple country with the tang of the apples in the air. We reached Verona early in the afternoon, tired and hungry, but happy. After dinner, some of us walked down to the main square of the town to sample the atmosphere. The square was filled with fountains and, of course, there was the famous amphitheatre. We strolled among the restaurants and cafés, with people sitting at tables on the pavement, drinking wine or cappuccino, and street music and jugglers providing entertainment. I would have loved to stay — for me, this was the real Italy.

The following morning, it was raining, and the weather forecast was bad. Having put on our rain-gear, we headed for Lido do Jesolo, 100 miles on main roads — not the cycling tracks we had been using. This turned out to be the worst day I have ever spent on a bike, with 35 m.p.h. winds, driving rain and the crazy Italian truck-drivers bearing down on us. I was really frightened. It can be difficult for a blind person to grasp what is going on around him, when there is a lot of noise. With the wind howling in my ears, I gritted my teeth and put my trust in Kevin to get us to the first food stop.

When we reached it, we were completely drenched — the rain had got in even under our rain-gear, my sandwich was soggy, my paper teacup disintegrating. I was miserable!

We had another 60 miles to go, and the management decided to carry on, so off we cycled into the storm, among those awful trucks. Then as Kevin and I were cycling along in a group, there was a twanging sound from the back wheel. The bike lurched, I jumped off, and we pulled in to the side of the road.

Three spokes had broken — the wheel would buckle if we rode any further. We decided to wait for our maintenance truck, and, as the rain came down even harder, we started to walk along the side of the road, pushing the tandem along, like two drowned rats. We had walked about three miles when the truck caught up with us. Fintan McGill had been brilliant throughout the trip, seeing that every bike was fit to go out each day, and he often worked late into the evening.

On this occasion, he decided that it was too wet to carry out repairs then and there, but one of the other tandem riders had had enough, so we were able to use his bike which was in the truck. We jumped on the borrowed tandem and headed after the group. We were a very long way behind and we hardly cared about the weather any more — we just wanted to catch up.

After an hour or so, the rain stopped and it got very hot, so we pulled in and stripped off our rain-gear, then took off again after the bunch. With twenty-five miles to go, we reached the second food stop, grabbed a drink of water, and chased after the group again. Then the heavens opened — huge drops — and in a moment we were soaked. On with the rain-gear again.

We caught up with the back of the bunch with ten miles to go, but I was suffering: my muscles ached, my bum was killing me. I was exhausted and still the rain poured down. Kevin encouraged me, joked, tried to make me laugh, but I was almost crying with the effort to pedal. Italian roads are bumpy and each bump was agony. 'Keep going, Joe,' I said to myself.

Suddenly when it was almost too much to bear, we reached Lido do Jesolo and the finishing line. Six hundred miles of gear-grinding, leg-aching, muscle-stretching, pushing, climbing, sliding, skidding, teeth-clenching cycling. And here we were — we had completed the whole bloody journey. I almost fell off the bike with relief. I felt so thankful for Kevin's support and encouragement — I hugged him, unable, for once, to speak.

* * *

I have now been on fund-raising cycle rides in California, Florida, Australia, Central Europe, South Africa and Canada.

On each trip, I had a different pilot, and some were better than others. To get a good tandem pair, you need to get on well with one another off the bike as well as on. The person on the back of the tandem is there only to provide the power. The pilot needs to have a good knowledge of cycling, and also to be able to describe things to the blind person on the back. It might seem obvious, but the pilot has to remember that the person behind can't see. I need to be helped when off the bike too, finding my way about in a hotel or ordering a meal at a self-service place. I can't point and say, 'I'll have that and that and that....'

Helping a blind person requires a certain kind of character. Everyone is eager to help at first, but two weeks on the road — and off it — can be stressful for some people, especially if this is the first blind person they've ever met.

~ Twenty-Five ~

Cycling around America made me ambitious, and in 1992, I decided to take off on my own and do a radio documentary for RTÉ. My purpose was to visit various European countries and find out what facilities were available for blind and visually impaired people.

Normally, I travel everywhere with Whiskey, but because of rabies regulations, I couldn't take her to the European mainland. I made arrangements for a guide to accompany me, but at the last moment, this person was unable to go with me.

I decided to call the documentary. *Around Europe Without My Dog*, and set off from Dublin one cold autumn day, alone.

I had made plans for people to meet me along the way, and knew more or less where I would be staying and with whom, but I must admit to being rather apprehensive. Most of those concerned were unknown to me, but fortunately I like meeting people. My itinerary was to take me to Belgium, the Netherlands, Luxembourg and Germany, and I hoped that everyone would be as helpful as the Aer Lingus employee who brought me to the plane in Dublin. He handed me over to an equally helpful hostess named Monica, who amazed me by handing me an emergency sheet in Braille. Sensibly enough, the document emphasised the importance of listening carefully to instructions and waiting to be told what to do by the cabin crew.

In Brussels, to my relief, Jean, the man who met me, spoke good English — my French is limited to '*Merci beaucoup*', '*Je ne parle pas le français*' and '*Je ne comprends pas*'. I did an interview, stayed in a hotel overnight and went next day to the 'League Braille'.

My overall recollections are of crowds, movement and

noise. I went down an escalator to the métro, found Marianne and Seán — *'Voilà!'* — and plunged into a noisy crowded labyrinth where I felt quite bewildered. Off the métro and into another taxi which took me to the Gare du Nord and my train to Amsterdam. Then I discovered that I was going not to Amsterdam but to the Hague. I sat in the station, anxiously waiting for the official who was to put me on the train, while I listened to the hubbub of the crowd and noticed a pleasant smell of pastry.

The journey was noisy and crowded like the station, and I listened as voices speaking French gave way to voices speaking Dutch — not that I understood either. Then at last we arrived and I was taken by taxi to my hotel. As I only stayed overnight in the Hague for the purpose of a brief meeting, I have no real recollection of the place. The changes that were made for me in my itinerary were rather confusing, and I was relieved when at last I set off to return to Brussels.

My problems weren't over though. The train was late, and finally broke down. I would have been helpless without the two passengers who grabbed my arms and practically dragged me across a bridge to the relief train. We just caught a train to Antwerp, thence back to Brussels.

At Brussels that night, four friends and I dined at an Italian restaurant, where I noticed that we were speaking five different languages: English, French, German, Italian and a wee bit of Spanish. It was a good evening, and next day, I set off for Luxembourg, a four-hour train journey.

I carried out three or four interviews in Luxembourg and realised how ill-informed I was about this small country, whose main industry is banking, and which has only 2.5 per cent unemployment. Next day, I left for Stuttgart, changing at Strasbourg.

At Strasbourg, an unfamiliar station, I stood on the platform for only a few seconds before three people asked if I needed help. They took me quite a distance to the platform where I was to catch the Stuttgart train.

I loved Stuttgart, and if I had to live in a German city, I think it would be Stuttgart. It was full of hustle and bustle, and the dialect sings along, with lots of strange words which aren't in High German at all. It was a happy, thriving place and, like me, people never stopped talking. When my work there was done, it was time to return to Ireland.

The first step was to catch a train to Brussels which left at 12.40 a.m. I had omitted to book a sleeping car, so I went to the 'Bahnhof Mission' to see if they could get me one. They couldn't, so I sat up for the whole trip of seven hours. I didn't sleep, as there was a drunken and noisy party of football supporters in the next compartment, and I was completely exhausted when I reached Brussels in the early morning.

Having been helped off the train, I made my way to a gate where I was to be met. While I waited, I folded up my white cane and put it away. Then, a woman's voice beside me asked the time. I consulted my talking watch and told her. She repeated her question and I realised she had said, 'Would you like a good time?' She was speaking German, and the word for 'time' misled me.

Fortunately, at that moment, my contact, Anne, rushed up and greeted me like a long-lost boyfriend. When the other woman had vanished, Anne turned to me and said, 'You're a right one — you've only been alone a few minutes and I find you talking to a lady of the night.'

I arrived home in Dublin, a week after I had left, pleased with having carried out my survey and got some good interviews. My conclusion was that many of the problems facing a blind person travelling in Europe are encountered by anyone unused to travelling, blind or otherwise. Anyone travelling abroad should learn a few phrases of the appropriate languages. Blind people *must* carry a white cane, and, above all, should never be afraid to ask for help.

There are huge differences from one country to another in what is available for blind people. In America they have so much going for them. They are fetched and carried, they have only to ask for something and it is provided. Of course, there is a lot more money available for provision of service for blind people in America than anywhere else.

In Europe without a guide, I never had to wait more than a few minutes with my white cane before help was offered — in Dutch, German or French. There was far more public awareness of the needs of a blind person, and less embarrassment in offering assistance than there is here.

There has been a great improvement in Ireland in the past ten years, but there is still a long way to go.

* * *

For many years, blindness was a cause for pity among those who could see. Pity is not the same thing as sympathy, which means a fellow feeling for somebody. Pity is an emotion which, although well meant, can be patronising. In the past few years, there have been big advances in the field of public awareness. People are learning. Of course there is still the person who says pityingly, 'Ah will you look at the poor blind man, God love him.' There are still those who think a blind person must be stone deaf, brainless, sexless and without any feelings.

Many adults are self-conscious and embarrassed in the company of a blind person — some never manage to be at their ease. Children are less inhibited though, and frequently ask, 'What is it like to be blind?'

It's wrong to imagine that a blind person lives in blackness — pitch darkness. There is simply an absence of any colour — 'A kind of no-colour nothingness,' to quote one child.

Going blind, for a person born with sight, is a profound shock as well as a loss. There can be nothing worse than gradually losing your sight. I lost mine suddenly and at a very young age, so I suppose that, up to a point, I took it for granted. I was lucky in having brothers and sisters around me. When I was at school in Liverpool, there was a girl there who could see, but was learning Braille because she was going to lose her sight, probably suddenly, quite soon. This girl had been told that she might wake up blind one day. She did when she was twelve years old.

While she could still see, she got an exercise book and painted pictures on every page. All the things she loved and would miss: green grass, blue sky, trees, flowers, people in bright coloured clothes. She filled the book, and every day she looked at all these pictures, trying to fix them in her mind.

For adults, loss of sight is different — the person has been educated, has probably got a job, a spouse. The loss is traumatic, and because of the sudden dependence on others and the sudden lack of mobility, the trauma is even greater. Life seems to have ended for such a person, and there is anger and resentment. It may take months or years for the person to come to terms with blindness and to make a new life.

I still resent being blind myself, although I came to terms with it many years ago. Everything is complicated and takes longer. Even with a guide dog, total independence is impossible. In a hotel bedroom, for example, I might think I'd like to go down to the bar. This would be too much for Whiskey to understand. She'd take me downstairs but then I'd have to ask somebody the way.

One of the few advantages, though, is a sense of achievement and wonder when you make a new discovery. I remember going to the zoo, and being given a baby chimpanzee to hold. It was a huge thrill. Another time, on a farm, I handled a sheep's newly shorn fleece and held a young lamb in my arms. What your eyes take in instantaneously takes much longer using only hearing, smell and touch.

Curiously also, much good has resulted from the loss of my sight as an infant, which seemed such a total calamity at the time. Because of it, I had many advantages which were not available to the rest of my family. Although I, a perpetually homesick boy, certainly didn't appreciate it at the time, my secondary education was invaluable to me. Had I not been blind, I might never have had the opportunity to use my talent for music, and I certainly wouldn't have been able to learn it from such an outstanding teacher — and personality — as Alan Mapson.

My travels have enabled me to visit many places which I would otherwise never have had the chance to see, and I have formed many lasting and worthwhile friendships. Latterly, I have had the opportunity to learn to help other blind and visually impaired people.

As for the future, I do have my dreams. I would like to write more, to compose more music, to do more radio work. One of my happiest times was when I presented my programme on pirate radio, but unfortunately I didn't get paid for it. I would like to present a radio show, playing the music I love, and I think perhaps there is an opening for this. For the present, it is just a dream.

* * *

In writing this book, I don't want anybody to suppose that I want to be taken as an example. What a person does with their life is up to them. I have simply told the story of what I have done with my life so far, in the hope that it will help sighted people to understand a little more. And if I have shown some blind and visually impaired people how fulfilled and happy a blind person's life can be, I won't have lived in vain.

Country Living
by Liz Kavanagh

From May Day nettle soup to mobile phones, from Eoin's PST (pre-silage tension) to the proper colour for wellies, from tussles with the Government to the trials and tribulations of bringing up five great boys — this is Liz Kavanagh at the top of her form!

For nearly twenty years, Liz Kavanagh has been delighting readers of the *Irish Farmers' Journal* with her weekly column — a feisty down-to-earth account of the many ups and downs of rural life.

Now, for the first time, Liz's best-loved columns have been brought together in book form.

It's all here: the wry humour, the sly descriptions of local characters, the childhood memories, the joys and disasters of life on a farm — all described with Liz Kavanagh's unique blend of wit and homespun wisdom.

ISBN 0-86327-609-1

Available from:
WOLFHOUND PRESS
68 Mountjoy Square
Dublin 1
Tel: +353 1 874 0354
Fax: +353 1 872 0207